The Original
Azusa Street
Devotional

The Original Azusa Street Devotional

HOUSE
A STRANG COMPANY

Larry Keefauver
General Editor

THE ORIGINAL AZUSA STREET DEVOTIONAL
Published by Charisma House
A Strang Company
600 Rinehart Road
Lake Mary, Florida 32746
www.charismahouse.com

Unless otherwise noted, all Scripture quotations are
from the King James Version of the Bible.

Library of Congress Cataloging-in-Publication Data
The Original Azusa Street Revival Devotional / Larry
Keefauver, general editor.
 1. Devotional calendars.   2. Christian life—
Pentecostal authors.
I. Keefauver, Larry.
ISBN: 0-88419-481-7
BV4810.O75 1997   242'.2—dc21   97-22328

06 07 08 09 — 9 8 7 6 5 4 3
Printed in the United States of America

Contents

Contents

Introduction

WILLIAM J. SEYMOUR had been an evangelist in Mississippi, then pastored a
Holiness congregation in Houston prior to his
arrival in Los Angeles in early 1906 to pastor
an African-American congregation led by Julia
W. Hutchins.

While in Mississippi, he was influenced by
people who had been under the ministry of
Charles Parham, a white minister in Topeka,
Kansas, who was called the founder of Pente-
costalism. Parham had founded a Bible School
where he and his students, starting with Agnes
M. Ozman, were baptized with the Spirit and
spoke in tongues.

Believing in the baptism of the Spirit with
the evidence of speaking in tongues, Seymour

provoked the ire of some of the congregation with his Pentecostal teaching. Not only did this bold, black evangelist preach holiness and divine healing at his church in Los Angeles, he also began preaching about the Holy Spirit's baptism. Locked out of the church one April evening, he was welcomed into the home of Mr. and Mrs. Edward Lee where he began conducting house meetings. On April 9, 1906, Seymour prayed for Lee's healing. Not only was Edward Lee healed, he also began speaking in tongues and started to testify to others about his experience. Later that same day, seven more people were baptized in the Spirit and spoke in tongues. On April 12, 1906, Seymour himself experienced the same baptism.

The interracial, integrated house meetings grew to such a size that they were moved to a two-story frame livery stable that had in its early days been a church building. By late April, the building, which could seat about 750 persons, was ready for meetings. Within days, revival broke out attracting people from all over the world. On April 18, 1906, the Los Angeles *Daily Times* reported the revival with a front-page story. During approximately one thousand days of revival, tens of thousands from around the world came to Azusa Street and were touched by the fiery outpouring of the Holy Spirit. This revival is considered by many to be the torch that ignited worldwide, Pentecostal revival in the twentieth century.

Pentecostal theology had its roots in nineteenth century fundamentalism with such key leaders as Charles Finney, R. A. Torrey, A. J. Gordon, and many others who spoke of the enduement of power by the Spirit, divine healing, and the imminent return of Christ. These Holiness streams led to a "four-square" emphasis of:

- Christ the Savior
- Christ the baptizer in the Holy Spirit
- Christ the healer
- Christ the coming King

These biblical themes are woven throughout *The Apostolic Faith* newsletter published by W. J. Seymour from the Azusa Street Revival. These remarkable newsletters spanned the first two years of the revival from September 1906, through May 1908.

Day 1

The Precious Atonement

And not only so, but we also joy in God through our Lord Jesus Christ, by whom we have now received the atonement.
—ROMANS 5:11

CHILDREN of God, partakers of the precious atonement, let us study and see what there is in it for us.

First, through the atonement we receive *forgiveness of sins.*

Second, we receive *sanctification* through the blood of Jesus. "Wherefore Jesus also, that he might sanctify the people with his own blood, suffered without the gate" (Heb. 13:12). Sanctified from all original sin, we become sons of God. "For both he that sanctifieth and they who are sanctified are all of one: for which cause he is not ashamed to call them brethren" (Heb. 2:11). It seems that Jesus would be ashamed to call them brethren if they were not sanctified. Then you will not be ashamed to tell men and demons that you are sanctified and are living a pure and holy life free from sin—a life that gives you power over the world, the flesh, and the devil.

Third, *healing* of our bodies. Sickness and disease are destroyed through the precious atonement of Jesus. Oh, how we ought to honor the stripes of Jesus, for "by whose stripes ye were healed" (1 Pet. 2:24; Isa. 53:5).

Not only is the atonement for the sanctification of our souls, but for the sanctification of our bodies from inherited disease. It matters not what has been in the blood. Every drop of blood we received from our mother is impure. Every sickness is of the devil. Jesus was manifested to destroy the works of the devil.

> *Thank You, Jesus, for Your precious blood of atonement. Sanctify, baptize, heal, and revive me with Your Holy Spirit. Amen.*

—W. J. SEYMOUR
SEPTEMBER 1906

Day 2

The Two Works of Grace

Then Peter said unto them, Repent, and be baptized every one of you in the name of Jesus Christ for the remission of sins, and ye shall receive the gift of the Holy Ghost.
—ACTS 2:38

WE PREACH old-time repentance, old-time conversion, old-time sanctification, and old-time baptism with the Holy Ghost which is the gift of power upon the sanctified life, and God throws in the gift of tongues.

Justification deals with our actual sins. When we go to God and repent, He washes all the guilt and pollution out of our hearts, and we stand justified like a new babe that never committed sin. We have no condemnation. If we walk in the Spirit, we can walk with Jesus and live a holy life before the Lord.

Sanctification is the second and last work of grace. After we are justified, we have two battles to fight. There is sin inside and sin outside. There is warfare within, caused by past, inherited sin. When God brings the Word, "This is the will of God, even your sanctification" (1 Thess. 4:3), we should accept the Word. Then His blood comes and takes away all inherited sin. Everything is heavenly in you—you are a child of God. The Spirit of God witnesses in your heart that you are sanctified.

The Spirit begins then and there leading us on to the *baptism with the Holy Ghost.*

As a child of God, you should enter into the earnest of your inheritance. After you have a clear witness of the two works of grace in your heart, receive this gift of God, which is a free gift without repentance. Pray for the power of the Holy Ghost, and God will give you a new language.

> *Jesus, baptize me with the power of Your Spirit. Amen.*

—SEPTEMBER 1906

Day 3

Marks of Fanaticism

*For God hath not called us unto unclean-
ness, but unto holiness. He therefore that
despiseth, despiseth not man, but God, who
hath also given unto us his holy Spirit.*
—1 THESSALONIANS 4:7–8

FANATICS are marked by harshness toward
those who do not fall in line with them,
and Jesus is not held up. Sooner or later the
fruits of the flesh appear in a lack of holy
living.

We note these things because some honest
souls have feared that this Pentecostal movement saw fanaticism. So we mark some of the
features of the meetings which are the opposite
of fanaticism. *Divine love to all,* especially to
the church, the body of Christ, of which every
justified soul is a member.

Humility. This is a humble work in a
humble place, and we are glad that it is. We
humble ourselves under the mighty hand of
God and constantly search the scriptures to

know His whole will and plan.

Holy lives. These people are living holy lives, separate from the world, the flesh, and the devil, and rescuing other souls to a life of purity and holiness. There is a Holy Ghost shine on the faces of the workers.

Is this the work of the devil? Friends, if you profess to know the Spirit of God and do not recognize Him when He comes, there is cause for you to be anxious about your own spiritual condition.

> *Sanctify me, Lord, that I might be holy as You are holy. Amen.*
> —OCTOBER 1906

Day 4

In Money Matters

Now concerning the collection for the saints . . . Upon the first day of the week let every one of you lay by him in store, as God hath prospered him.

—1 CORINTHIANS 16:1–2

THERE HAVE BEEN teachers who have told all the people to sell out, and many of them have gone into fanaticism. We let the Spirit lead people and tell them what they ought to give.

When they get filled with the Spirit, their pocket books are converted, and God makes them stewards. If God says, "Sell out," they will do so. But sometimes they have families. God does not tell you to forsake your family. He says if you do not provide for your own you are worse than an infidel (1 Tim. 5:8).

Under false teaching, children have been left to go half-naked, women have left their husbands, and husbands leave their wives to wash and scrub. The Bible says that is worse than infidelity. Then they will go and borrow and cannot pay back. That person ought to go to work.

God does not expect you to sell out everything, forsaking your obligations. His Word does not mean for you to have great real estate and money banked up while your brothers and sisters are suffering. He means for you to turn loose, because all that money is soon going to be thrown to the moles and bats. So it is better to spread the gospel and get stars in your crown than to be holding on to your money.

God wants a free giver. The Spirit will tell you what to do. When He wakes you up at night and tells you what to do, you cannot sleep until you obey.

> *Lord, I want to hear from You concerning my giving and finances. Instruct me how to give. Amen.*

—W. J. SEYMOUR
NOVEMBER 1906

Day 5

Honor the Holy Ghost

Quench not the Spirit. Despise not prophesyings. Prove all things; hold fast to that which is good.

—1 THESSALONIANS 5:19–21

HONOR the Holy Ghost. Do not quench the Spirit. It is not you that speaks but the Holy Ghost, and He will speak when He chooses.

Don't you ever try to speak with tongues or say that the power belongs to you. "It is by my Spirit," saith the Lord (Zech. 4:6). He wants you to pray for the interpretation, so that you can speak with the Spirit and with the understanding also (1 Cor. 14:15).

I honor You, Holy Spirit, with my thoughts, words, and actions. Amen.

—MAY 1908

Day 6

The Heavenly Anthem

*Praise ye the Lord. Sing unto the Lord a
new song, and his praise in the congregation of saints.*

—P<small>SALM</small> 149:1

ONE OF THE most remarkable features of
this Apostolic Faith movement is what is
rightly termed the heavenly anthem. No one
but those who are baptized with the Holy
Ghost are able to join in—or better, the
Holy Ghost only sings through such in that
manner. Hallelujah!

"I have heard and understood, both in the
Gujerathi and Hindustant languages, the
singing of different psalms and other portions
of the holy Scriptures. The singing is done in
various foreign languages" (George E. Berg of
Hermon, California, a former missionary to
India).

On Sunday night, December 9, a sister sang
the first four verses of the eighth chapter of

Solomon's Songs in the Gujerathi language of India. It was a song such as a bride might sing of the bridegroom. "Awake not, my beloved." It was most blessed and beautiful to notice as the Holy Spirit sang through the dear sister. It brought a great wave of heavenly fire and blessing to those present.

Again a beautiful song was sung in tongues, "Hosanna to the Son of David: Blessed is he that cometh in the name of the Lord; Hosanna in the highest" (Matt. 21:9). The brother who understood the language said it was the sublimest poetry in the foreign tongue. At the same time, the room was filled with the glory of God.

We afterward learned of a remarkable coincidence. The same song was being sung at the Pentecostal Mission at 327½ S. Spring Street, and was interpreted there the same. The saints worshiping in these two places were in perfect harmony of spirit, and the Holy Ghost witnessed to it.

To You, Oh, Lord, I sing a new song of praise, lifting up my voice in adoration and rejoicing. Amen.

—JANUARY 1907

Day 7

Old Testament Feasts Today

Therefore let us keep the feast, not with old leaven, neither with the leaven of malice and wickedness; but with the unleavened bread of sincerity and truth.
—1 CORINTHIANS 5:8

IN THE TWENTY-THIRD chapter of Leviticus and sixteenth chapter of Deuteronomy, and all through the Old Testament, we read of the feasts that God appointed to be kept in worship to Him.

There were four feasts: the Passover Feast, Feast of First Fruits, Feast of Pentecost (or Feast of Weeks), and Feast of Tabernacles. They typify what we get through the cross now, justification, sanctification, the baptism with the Holy Ghost, and then a continual feast. Together they typify a complete redemption.

The Passover Feast is the type of justification through the blood of Jesus, our Paschal Lamb. The night they ate the Passover in Egypt was the type of a sinner coming out of darkness through the blood of Jesus. Hallelujah! The body of the Paschal Lamb is the type of the body of Christ, which is meat and bread for us, and the sprinkled blood represents salvation, as He said on that last Passover night when He was betrayed. "This is my body which is given for you: this do in remembrance of me" (Luke 22:19). He also gave them the cup, saying, "This cup is the new testament in my blood, which is shed for you" (Luke 22:20).

The Passover represents justification and sanctification. There is a feast in every believer who has accepted the blood of Jesus Christ. It is the first feast in his soul. When a man gets justified, the Lord puts a new song in his mouth, even praises to our God that he is saved and has peace with God through the blood of Jesus.

> *Paschal Lamb of God, pass me over*
> *from death to life by the redemption of*
> *Your blood. Amen.*

—JUNE–SEPTEMBER 1907

Day 8

I Know Thy Works

Nevertheless, I have somewhat against thee, because thou hast left thy first love.
—REVELATION 2:4

JESUS SAID, God knows our works. He knows our hearts. "I know thy works, and thy labour, and thy patience, and how thou canst not bear them which are evil: and thou hast tried them which say they are apostles, and are not, and hast found them liars: and hast borne, and hast patience, and for my name's sake hast laboured, and hast not fainted" (Rev. 2:2–3).

That Word is more than many churches today could receive from the Master. Jesus commended them for what they had done. He is not like men. He knows our hearts, trials, and conditions. Jesus does not make any allowance for sin. He hates sin today as much as He ever did. Yet He does not come to destroy us or condemn us, but to seek and to save us.

The Lord does not want anything to come between us and Him. May every precious child in these times that are getting the Holy Spirit not go into apostasy, but may they be a burning and a shining light for God, just as we were when we first received the baptism with the Holy Spirit. God wants us to keep the same anointing that we received and let nothing separate us from Christ.

> *Jesus, You are my first love. Keep me burning passionately hot for You. Amen.*

—OCTOBER–JANUARY 1908

Day 9

The Holy Ghost Is Power

And my speech and my preaching was not with enticing words of man's wisdom, but in demonstration of the Spirit and of power.

—1 Corinthians 2:4

THERE IS A great difference between a sanctified person and one that is baptized with the Holy Ghost and fire. A sanctified person is cleansed and filled with divine love, but the one that is baptized with the Holy Ghost has the power of God on his soul and has power with God and men, power over all the kingdoms of Satan and over all his emissaries.

In all Jesus' great revivals and miracles, the work was wrought by the power of the Holy Ghost flowing through His sanctified humanity. When the Holy Ghost comes and takes us as His instruments, this is the power that convicts men and women and causes them to see that there is a reality in serving Jesus Christ.

Oh, beloved, we ought to thank God that

He has made us the tabernacles of the Holy Ghost. When you have the Holy Ghost, you have an empire, a power within yourself.

The Lord never revoked the commission He gave to His disciples: "Heal the sick, cleanse the lepers, raise the dead. . . ." (Matt. 10:8). Jesus is going to perform these things through us if He can get a people in unity.

Jesus said, "Behold, I give unto you power to tread on serpents and scorpions, and over all the powers of the enemy" (Luke 10:19).

> *Through me, Lord, heal the sick, cleanse the lepers, raise the dead, cast out devils, and freely use all I have to minister. Amen.*

—MAY 1908

Day 10

Continual Revival

Repent ye therefore, and be converted, that your sins may be blotted out, when the times of refreshing shall come from the presence of the Lord.

—ACTS 3:19

THE BAPTISM of the Spirit is the infilling of the personal Holy Ghost, which is the earnest of the Spirit.

Then God gives us the authority to do the same work that Jesus did. We find where men and women have received this baptism with the Spirit there is a revival going on, just as on the day of Pentecost. That is what the baptism of the Spirit means—continual revival.

Holy Spirit, baptize and revive me continually so that I might live in Your revival. Amen.

Day 11

The Body of Christ

And whether one member suffer, all the members suffer with it; or one member be honoured, all members rejoice with it. Now ye are the body of Christ. . . .
—1 CORINTHIANS 12:26–27

IF YOU WANT to see God work in power, see a people that are living in love, unity, and harmony. But if the devil can get in and divide the people of God and sow dissension among them, then God cannot work.

Every blood-washed soul is a member of the body. We cannot reject one without hurting the whole body. All believers are important to the body of Christ.

> *Jesus, help me rejoice with others in the body, and comfort others when they suffer. Amen.*

—JANUARY 1907

Day 12

Enter the Holy of Holies

Having therefore, brethren, boldness to enter into the holiest by the blood of Jesus, by a new and living way, which he hath consecrated for us.

—HEBREWS 10:19–20

HEN WE enter into the Holy of Holies by the blood of Jesus, we encounter the ark of the covenant which is overshadowed by the wings of the cherubim.

Over the ark is the great Shekinah glory, a pillar of fire by night and a cloud by day, which represents the baptism with the Holy Spirit. There is no altar in the Holy of Holies, for our consecration is all made in the Holy Place when we are sanctified. We find the ark of the covenant covered with pure gold, and within, Aaron's rod that budded, which stands for justification in Christ Jesus. Also the pot of manna which Moses hid in the ark represents sanctification, and he put in it the tables of stone on which God wrote Himself on the mount. The ark represents the baptism with the Holy Ghost, for when we are baptized with the Holy Spirit we are sealed until His coming.

Here the great Shekinah glory rests upon us day and night, and we are filled and thrilled with the power of the Holy Spirit. The incense is going up continually from our souls. In the Holy Place, the oil was renewed from day to day, but when we get the baptism with the Holy Ghost it oils us up continually from the throne of God. In the Holy Place we had the streams of salvation. But in the Holy of Holies, we have the rivers, for Jesus said, "Out of his belly shall flow rivers of living water" (John 7:38–39).

> *Lord, make me a tabernacle for Your*
> *Spirit like the tabernacle of old. Fill*
> *me with Your Shekinah glory. Amen.*
> —DECEMBER 1906

Day 13

Praying for the Holy Ghost

*If ye then, being evil, know how to give
good gifts unto your children: how much
more shall your heavenly Father give the
Holy Spirit to them that ask him?*

—LUKE 11:13

E ARE NOW hearing from individuals
and companies who are definitely waiting
on God for their personal Pentecost. Some
have been stimulated in seeking by hearing of
God's visitation in Los Angeles. We join hands
with all such hungry seekers and meet you at
the throne.

Before another issue of this paper, we look
for Brother Parham in Los Angeles, a brother
who is full of divine love and whom the Lord
raised up five years ago to spread this truth.
He, with other workers, will hold union revival
meetings in Los Angeles, and then expects to
go on to other towns and cities, and will appoint
workers to fill the calls that come in.

Begin to pray right away for a revival in

your neighborhood or town or city. Perhaps you need one in your own closet or at your family altar first. But expect great things from God. Begin to prepare for a revival—a great and deep revival—and believe for it. It may cost you money, and it may humble you, but prepare for the Lord's coming.

> *God, send revival to my life, my family, and my town. Revive me that I might be a torch to revive others. Amen.*
>
> —OCTOBER 1906

Day 14

Sanctification and Power

I pray not that thou shouldest take them out of the world, but that thou shouldest keep them from the evil. They are not of the world, even as I am not of the world.
—JOHN 17:15–16

AVE YOU accepted Jesus? Will you accept Him? Have you accepted Him as your sanctifier? "This is the will of God, even your sanctification" (1 Thess. 4:3). Bless His dear name. He says, "Behold, I stand at the door, and knock: if any man hear my voice, and open the door, I will come in to him, and will sup with him, and he with me" (Rev. 3:20). Oh, let us invite Jesus into our hearts today that He might be our invited guest, and we shall sup with Him and He with us. Praises to our God. Hosanna to His omnipotent name!

If we are sanctified and have clean hearts, living pure, holy lives, and having perfect love in our souls, Oh, let us then receive the baptism with the Holy Ghost—the promise of the Father—that we may be able to be His witnesses in Jerusalem, Judea, and Samaria, and unto the uttermost parts of the earth. For Jesus gave this great commission in His resurrection power, after He rose from the dead. "Go ye therefore, and teach all nations, baptizing them in the name of the Father, and of the Son, and of the Holy Ghost: Teaching them to observe all things whatsoever I have commanded you: and, lo, I am with you alway, even unto the end of the world" (Matt. 28:19–20).

His great desire on the cross was for the salvation of souls.

Lord, give me a passion for forgiveness
and for lost souls. Amen.

—November 1906

Day 15

Virtue in the Perfect Body

Whoso eateth my flesh, and drinketh my blood, hath eternal life; and I will raise him up at the last day.

—JOHN 6:54

JESUS GAVE His perfect eyes for us, perfect hearing, perfect smelling, tasting, and feeling; for Jesus gave a perfect body that laid in the tomb three days and three nights, and was raised by the power of the Holy Ghost. Those eyes that had slept in the tomb under the great power of death were quickened and brought to life again by the power of the Holy Ghost. So, through the perfect body of our Lord Jesus Christ, we can receive perfect healing of sight, hearing, tasting, and smelling.

The Jews said, "How can this man give us his flesh to eat?" (v. 52).

Then Jesus said unto them, "Verily, verily, I say unto you, Except ye eat the flesh of the Son of man, and drink his blood, ye have no life in you" (v. 53). Oh. how true this is. May we drink His blood daily and eat His flesh through faith in His Word for salvation, health, and healing. If His flesh had seen corruption, then we could not have healing for the body nor look for an immortal body in heaven.

So dear beloved, we get healing for our body, soul, and spirit and an immortal body in heaven at His coming, through the perfect body of Jesus. Praise our God!

> *Jesus, You are the bread of life for me.*
> *I eat Your living bread and receive life*
> *from You. I give You praise for Your*
> *perfect body. Amen.*
> —FEBRUARY–MARCH 1907

Day 16

Feast of First Fruits

When ye be come into the land which I give unto you, and shall reap the harvest thereof, then ye shall bring a sheaf of the firstfruits of your harvest unto the priest.

—LEVITICUS 23:10

THIS IS THE very type of consecrating our lives, after we are justified, to be sanctified. Praise our God! Jesus Christ is our high priest. He sanctifies and cleanses us from all sin through His blood. Bless His holy name!

"And the meat offering thereof shall be two tenth deals of fine flour mingled with oil, an offering made by fire unto the Lord for a sweet savour: and the drink offering thereof shall be of wine, the fourth part of a hin. And ye shall eat neither bread, nor parched corn, nor green ears, until the selfsame day that ye have brought an offering unto your God: it shall be a statute for ever throughout your generations in all your dwellings" (Lev. 23:13–14). This is the very type of a fully sanctified life. We should not live off the experience and blessings of justification. But we should hasten to God as soon as we are justified, consecrating our whole soul to God as a sacrifice, and receive the sanctifying grace.

> *Lord, I surrender all my life to You*
> *and give You the first fruits of all that*
> *I receive from You. Amen.*

—JUNE–SEPTEMBER 1907

Day 17

Repentance

For godly sorrow worketh repentance to salvation not to be repented of: but the sorrow of the world worketh death.
—2 CORINTHIANS 7:10

WE FIND Jesus still preaches the same doctrine of repentance that He preached while on earth. "From that time Jesus began to preach, and to say, 'Repent: for the kingdom of heaven is at hand'" (Matt. 4:17).

In order to get right with God, He says, "Remember therefore from whence thou art fallen, and repent, and do the first works; or else I will come unto thee quickly, and will remove thy candlestick out of his place, except thou repent" (Rev. 2:5).

If there is anything wrong in your life and Jesus has His finger upon it, Oh, may you give it up, for Jesus is truly in His church today. This is the Holy Ghost dispensation, and He does convince men of sin, righteousness, and the judgment, and if we will be honest, God will bless us.

> *Lord, I repent of my sinful ways and ask that Your blood cleanse me and make me pure. Amen.*
> —OCTOBER–JANUARY 1908

Tarry in One Accord

*And suddenly there came a sound from
heaven as of a rushing mighty wind, and it
filled all the house where they were sitting.*
—ACTS 2:2

AY EVERY CHILD of God seek his real
personal Pentecost. We must stop quib-
bling and come to the standard that Jesus laid
down for us. Wait on God for this baptism of
the Holy Ghost just now.

Gather two or three people together who
are sanctified through the blood of Christ. Get
into one accord, and God will send the baptism of the Holy Ghost upon your souls as the
rain falls from heaven.

You may not have a preacher to come to
you and preach the doctrine of the Holy
Ghost and fire, but you can obey Jesus' saying
in the passage, "Where two or three are gathered together in my name, there am I in the
midst of them" (Matt. 18:20).

This is Jesus' baptism—and if two or three gather together in His name and pray for the baptism of the Holy Ghost, they can have it this day or this night, because it is the promise of the Father. Glory to God!

This was the Spirit that filled the house as a mighty rushing wind. The Holy Ghost is typified by wind, air, breath, life, and fire. "And there appeared unto them cloven tongues like as of fire, and it sat upon each of them. And they were all filled with the Holy Ghost, and began to speak with other tongues, as the Spirit gave them utterance" (Acts 2:3–4).

So, beloved, when you get your personal Pentecost, the signs will follow in speaking with tongues as the Spirit gives utterance. This is true. Wait on God and you will find it a truth in your own life. God's promises are true and sure.

> *Lord, as we gather in one accord waiting upon You, pour out Pentecost and revival upon us. Amen.*

—MAY 1908

Day 19

The Baptism's Real Evidence

*Though I speak with the tongues of men
and of angels, and have not charity, I am
become as sounding brass, or a tinkling
cymbal.*

—1 CORINTHIANS 13:1

THE REAL EVIDENCE that a man or woman
has received the baptism of the Holy
Ghost is divine love, which is charity. That
person will have the fruit of the Spirit.

"But the fruit of the Spirit is love, joy, peace,
long suffering, gentleness, goodness, faith,
meekness, temperance: against such there is no
law. And they that are Christ's have crucified
the flesh with the affections and lusts" (Gal.
5:22–24).

The fruit of the Spirit is the real Bible evidence in their daily walk and conversation.
The outward manifestations of the Spirit's
baptism are speaking in tongues and signs following: casting out devils; laying hands on the
sick and the sick being healed; and the love of

God for souls increasing in their hearts (Mark 16:15–18).

> *Lord, grow Your fruit in my life. Amen.*

—JANUARY 1908

Day 20

Lies

Beloved, believe not every spirit, but try the spirits whether they are of God . . . Every spirit that confesseth that Jesus Christ is come in the flesh is of God.

—1 JOHN 4:1–2

THE LORD WILL hold you just as responsible for believing a lie as He did Adam. False doctrine kills the soul. If we get out of the Word of God and believe a lie, we lose the blood and lose the life out of our souls.

Let no one deceive you, not even if he comes as an angel of light, nor your own church nor pastor if they get you to doubt the Word and believe a lie.

God's Word tells us: "For such are false apostles, deceitful workers, transforming themselves into the apostles of Christ. And no marvel; for Satan himself is transformed into an angel of light. Therefore it is no great thing if his ministers also be transformed as the ministers of righteousness; whose end shall be according to their works" (2 Cor. 11:13–15).

> *Spirit of Truth, teach me the Word*
> *and guard me from every lie and false*
> *doctrine. Amen.*

—JANUARY 1907

Day 21

The Polishing Process

*But we all, with open face beholding as in
a glass the glory of the Lord, are changed
into the same image from glory to glory,
even as by the Spirit of the Lord.*
—2 CORINTHIANS 3:18

SEVERAL YEARS AGO, when I was very hungry,
seeking God in all His fullness, I shut
myself away in my closet one day, and the
Lord gave me a wonderful revelation. As I was
kneeling before my Maker, beseeching Him to
show me all He expected me to be, right
before my eyes I saw this wonderful vision.
There appeared a man with a large, long,
knotty, but straight log. The man had an ax.

Did you ever see anybody score timber? He
was scoring the log, and it seemed to me the ax
went clear to the bit. And every time he
scored, it hurt me. He scored it on four sides
and then took the broad ax and whacked off
the knots. Then he took a line and with an adz
he made it pretty smooth. Then he raised it in

the air, and taking a great plane, turned to me and said, "This is the plane of the Holy Ghost." He ran the plane up and down, until I could see the image of the man perfectly reflected in the face of the log, as in a mirror. He did this to all four sides. Then turning to me, he said: "Thou art all fair, my love; there is no spot in thee" (Song of Sol. 4:7).

That is what God wants to do with us. He wants to take all the bumps, all the barnacles off. We have only begun to lay ourselves on the anvil of God's truth. The hammer is being applied to us. He may have to throw us back in the smelter several times. Let us stay in the fire until there is no more dross in us.

Let us stay on the anvil of God until we reflect the image of the Master.

> *Lord, transform me by Your Spirit*
> *that I might reflect Your glory. Amen.*
> —MRS. ANNA HALL
> OCTOBER 1906

Day 22

Back to Pentecost

For thus saith the Lord God; Behold, I, even I, will both search my sheep, and seek them out.

—EZEKIEL 34:11

WHAT IS the meaning of these salaried preachers over the land that will not preach unless they get so much salary? People have wandered from the old landmarks. The priests had no land of their own. They were to live on the tithes and offerings. The ministers of today have wandered from the old landmarks. Therefore they are seeking salary over the land. Get back. You have no time to lose.

Do you want to be blest? Do you want the approbation of God? Be a servant to humanity. The loaves and fishes did not multiply in the hands of our blessed Redeemer until He began to give out to the hungry. God does not need a great theological preacher that can give nothing but theological chips and shavings to people. He takes the weak things to confound the mighty. He can pick up a worm and thrash a mountain. He is picking up pebble stones from the street and polishing them for His work. He is using even the children to preach His gospel.

A young sister, fourteen years old, was saved, sanctified, and baptized with the Holy Ghost and went out, taking a band of workers with her, and led a revival in which one hundred ninety souls were saved. Salaried ministers that are rejecting the gospel will have to go out of business. He is sending out those who will go without money and without price.

Jesus, I pray for the shepherds who feed the bread of life to Your sheep. Preserve and keep them.

—OCTOBER 1906

Day 23

Salvation and Healing

And the very God of peace sanctify you wholly; and I pray God your whole spirit and soul and body be preserved blameless unto the coming of our Lord Jesus Christ.
—1 Thessalonians 5:23

THROUGH JESUS we are entitled to health and sanctification of soul and body. We have just as much right to look to Jesus for the health of these bodies as for the saving and sanctifying of our souls.

The sacrifice on Calvary was a two-fold sacrifice. When we receive the atonement in all its fullness, we have health and salvation to the uttermost. It is by the stripes of Jesus that we are healed (Isa. 53:5). Pilate scourged Jesus before the judgment bar. The marks that were made on that perfect body of our Savior, the blood that ran down in Pilate's judgment hall from His stripes, reaches our infirmities and cleanses us from all sickness and disease making us every whit whole.

The Passover lamb was a type of Christ. We find that God commanded the children of Israel, when they were about to come out of Egypt, to take a lamb without blemish and kill it and sprinkle the blood at the doors of their homes, and eat the body of the lamb in their houses. The blood stood for salvation to save them from the destroyer. The blood of Jesus saves us from sin, for Satan is not able to make his way through the blood.

Let us take the Lamb's body, through faith in our Lord, for salvation and healing of these bodies, as we honor His blood for saving and sanctifying our soul and spirit. Amen.

Jesus, by Your stripes I am healed. I receive the healing in Your blood. Amen.

—NOVEMBER 1906

Day 24

Digging for Oil

As the hart panteth after the water brooks, so panteth my soul after thee, Oh, God. My soul thirsteth for God, for the living God.

—PSALM 42:1–2

I ONCE ASKED a man who was digging oil wells, how he found the oil. He said, "We bore down six to eight hundred feet until we strike the rock. Then we bore through that rock about five feet, and on down to the second rock, about three feet thinner than the first. Then we strike a lake of oil."

It reminded me of salvation. Digging down to the rock represents repentance. When you get through all the dirt and mud and strike the rock, that represents salvation in Christ, for Christ is the Rock. But when we get upon the rock, we have to build.

The man said they had to bore through two rocks before they struck the lake of oil. It reminded me of the two works of grace. We cross the Red Sea, then Jordan, and then we receive our inheritance. Elisha crossed Jordan and looked up into heaven as Elijah was caught up in the chariot of fire, and the mantle of Elisha fell upon Elisha. This is a type of receiving the baptism with the Holy Ghost, for Elijah prayed for a double portion of the spirit of Elijah (see 2 Kings 2:9).

The second rock represents the second work of grace, sanctification. You go down through that rock and strike the lake of oil and it gushes out in plenty. The oil represents the baptism with the Holy Ghost. Some get the anointing and are filled with holy laughter, and take that to be the baptism. But if we go on through that other rock, we will get to the lake of oil.

God, I long for You. I seek all that You have for me and all of You. Amen.
—FEBRUARY–MARCH 1907

The Feast of Pentecost

And there appeared unto them cloven tongues like as of fire, and it sat upon each of them. And they were all filled with the Holy Ghost.

—ACTS 2:3–4

THE FEAST OF Pentecost is the very type of the baptism with the Holy Ghost. The word *Pentecost* signifies fifty days. The first Pentecost the Jews had was at Mount Sinai fifty days after the Feast of Passover.

The baptism with the Holy Ghost also fell on Pentecost just fifty days after Jesus was offered on the cross. The regular time of offering the lamb of sacrifice was nine o'clock, and that was the hour that Jesus was crucified—the third hour of the day. And the baptism of the Spirit fell at the same hour, fifty days later.

In the second chapter of Acts, we read that Peter said to the multitude, "These are not drunken, as ye suppose, seeing it is but the third hour of the day" (Acts 2:15).

The Pentecost fell on the Lord's day, the first day of the week or Sunday. It has been kept by God's people ever since. Pentecost really means a feast; praise God, we have Pentecost today.

The feast of Pentecost came at the time of the wheat harvest and ripening of the summer fruits. They were commanded to leave some of the wheat and fruits in the fields, not to glean it. When we get the baptism with the Holy Ghost, we have overflowing love, we have rivers of salvation. Praise our God.

> *Oh God, pour out Your Pentecost in my life. Amen.*

—JUNE–SEPTEMBER 1907

Day 26

Impure Doctrine

For the time will come when they will not endure sound doctrine; but after their own lusts, shall they heap to themselves teachers, having itching ears.

—2 TIMOTHY 4:3

WE FIND MANY of Christ's people tangled up in these days, committing spiritual fornication as well as physical fornication and adultery. They say, "Let us all come together, if we are not one in doctrine, we can be one in spirit." But, dear ones, we cannot all be one, except through the word of God. He says, "But this thou hast, that thou hatest the deeds of the Nicolaitans, which I also hate" (Rev. 2:6). I suppose that the apostolic church at Ephesus allowed people that were not teaching straight doctrine, not solid in the Word of God, to remain in fellowship with them. Jesus knew that a little leaven would leaven the whole, and His finger was right upon that impure doctrine. It had to be removed out of the church or He would remove the light and break the church up.

When we find things wrong, contrary to Scripture, I care not how dear it is—it must be removed. We cannot bring Agag among the children of Israel, for God says he must die. Saul saved Agag, which represented saving himself, the carnal nature or old man, but Samuel said Agag must die, and he drew his sword and slew him (1 Sam. 15).

Christ's precious Word puts all carnality and sin to death. It means perfect obedience to walk with the Lord. The Lord says, "He that hath an ear, let him hear what the Spirit saith unto the churches; To him that overcometh will I give to eat of the tree of life" (Rev. 2:7).

In You, Lord Jesus, I am an overcomer. Keep my thoughts and doctrine pure, according to Your Word. Amen.

—W. J. SEYMOUR
OCTOBER–JANUARY 1908

Day 27

The Baptism of a Clean Heart

And Jesus being full of the Holy Ghost returned from Jordan, and was led by the Spirit into the wilderness.

—LUKE 4:1

JESUS IS OUR example. Upon His clean heart, the baptism fell. We find in reading the Bible that the baptism with the Holy Ghost and fire falls on a clean, sanctified life. For we see according to the Scriptures that Jesus was filled with wisdom and favor with God and man, before God anointed Him with the Holy Ghost and power. For in Luke 2:40, we read that, "[Jesus] waxed strong in spirit, filled with wisdom: and the grace of God was upon Him." Then in Luke 2:52, "And Jesus increased in wisdom and stature, and in favour with God and man."

After Jesus was empowered with the Holy Ghost at Jordan, He returned in the power of the Spirit into Galilee, and there went out a fame of Him through all the region round about. He was not any more holy or any more meek, but had greater authority. "And he taught in their synagogues, being glorified by all" (Luke 4:15).

Beloved, if Jesus, who was God Himself, needed the Holy Ghost to empower Him for His ministry and His miracles, how much more do we children need the Holy Ghost baptism today. Oh that men and women would tarry for the baptism with the Holy Ghost and fire upon their souls!

The tongues of fire represented the great Shekinah glory. Today the Shekinah glory rests day and night upon those who are baptized with the Holy Ghost, while He abides in their souls. For His presence is with us.

> *God, cleanse my heart with Your fire*
> *that I may receive the baptism of Your*
> *Spirit. Amen.*

—MAY 1908

Day 28

A Pure and Holy Life

For both he that sanctifieth and they who are sanctified are all of one: for which cause he is not ashamed to call them brethren.

—Hebrews 2:11

I
N ORDER TO live a pure and holy life one does not need the baptism of the Holy Ghost. The Holy Ghost does not cleanse anyone from sin. It is Jesus' shed blood on Calvary that cleanses us from sin. The Holy Ghost never died for our sins. It was Jesus who died for our sins, and it is His blood that atones.

"If we walk in the light, as he is in the light, we have fellowship one with another, and the blood of Jesus Christ his Son cleanseth us from all sin. . . . If we confess our sins, he is faithful and just to forgive us our sins, and to cleanse us from all unrighteousness" (1 John 1:7, 9). It is the blood that cleanses and makes holy, and through the blood we receive the baptism of the Holy Spirit. The Holy Ghost always falls in response to the blood.

> *Jesus, cleanse and purify me with Your blood. Amen.*

—JANUARY 1908

Day 29

We Must Humble Ourselves

*Whosoever therefore shall humble himself
as this little child, the same is greatest in
the kingdom of heaven.*
—MATTHEW 18:4

SOME SAY that it takes little "thimble-brained" people to accept this gospel. We have so much unbelief that we must be emptied out before we can be filled. The one that does not know any more than just to believe God, gets down and takes Him at His Word, and the witness comes that the blood of Jesus does save and sanctify from all sin. In faith the believer trusts the promises of the Father, receives the baptism of the Holy Spirit, and receives the Bible evidence of that. It is now, as in the time of Christ, when the people heard Him gladly.

The Greeks required knowledge and the Jews a sign, but the simple-hearted people just believed Jesus. The Lord has such people today that are following the Lamb whithersoever He goeth.

May God help us to humble ourselves to receive all that the Holy Ghost has for us.

> *Jesus, I desire all that Your Spirit has for me. I trust Your Word. Humble me so that I may receive all. Amen.*

Day 30

Contend for the Faith

Beloved, [I] exhort you that ye should earnestly contend for the faith which was once delivered unto the saints.

—JUDE 1:3

IT IS OUR PRIVILEGE to contend earnestly for the power that was in the early apostolic church—so that men will be instantly healed and baptized with the Holy Ghost. The power of God is going to fall on men in our cities.

God wants people who will believe in Him and exercise the faith. Faith moves God. Faith is one thing that gets results with God (Heb. 11).

When they put Paul and Silas in the Philippian jail, they went joyfully (Acts 16). They sang and prayed and at midnight God heard their prayers in heaven and shook the earth until the doors flew open. The jailer trembled and was going to take his life. But he fell under conviction. What happened? All were saved.

When those men called upon God, something happened. I believe those men had faith in God. When are we going to get that perfect faith? The Lord is just preparing His people now for the work He is going to do. We have been a great distance from His work. The devil does not like to see us victorious, but Satan has already been defeated by God. Believers who contend for the faith are overcomers. They are more than conquerors in Christ Jesus.

In You, Lord Jesus, I place my faith. I contend for the faith that moves mountains and touches the Father's heart. Revive me with miracle-working faith. Amen.

—SEPTEMBER 1906

Day 31

The Baptism Foreshadowed

Let them make me a sanctuary; that I may dwell among them.

—Exodus 25:8

DEAR LOVED ONES, the Lord Jesus is the true tabernacle that God pitched and not man. The tabernacle in the wilderness was made after the pattern of the heavenly tabernacle which God showed Moses in the holy mount. We now have the true pattern which is the Lord Jesus Christ, the Son of the living God.

We first come to the court of the tabernacle where we find the brazen altar, where whole burnt offerings are made. When we first came, we were dead in our sins and could make no offering for we had no life in our souls.

Jesus pardons us of our sins and plants the new birth in our souls.

Then we go on to the Holy Place to consecrate ourselves. There we find the believer's altar which is the golden altar. We sanctify ourselves and consecrate ourselves to God as a living sacrifice, and we find the precious blood in the Holy Place that sanctifies and cleanses us from all sin, crucifies the old man, the body of sin and carnality, and makes us holy. We had to have eternal life in our souls in order to consecrate ourselves. Here we feed upon Christ, for the bread in the Holy Place typifies the bread of life. "Man shall not live by bread alone, but by every word that proceedeth out of the mouth of God" (Matt. 4:4). Here also is the golden candlestick that sheds its light continually day and night, supplied by the holy oil. We are now the sons and daughters of God and entitled to the earnest of our inheritance, which is the baptism with the Holy Spirit.

Dwell in me, Oh, glory of the Living Spirit. Sanctify and cleanse my spirit and make me holy. Amen.

—DECEMBER 1906

Day 32

Healing

Is any sick among you? let him call for the elders of the church; and let them pray over him, anointing him with oil in the name of the Lord.

—JAMES 5:14

JESUS STILL heals today. Praise God! Jesus said, "Men ought always to pray and not to faint" (Luke 18:1). Many precious children of God today, instead of praying, commence grieving. But God's Word says, "Let him pray." And if we obey His Word, He will heal us. We read in Psalm 107:20, "He sent his word, and healed them, and delivered them from their destructions." And we read in Proverbs 4:20, "My son, attend to my words; incline thine ear unto my sayings."

Jesus is speaking through the power of the Holy Ghost to every believer to keep His precious Word. "Let them not depart from thine eyes; keep them in the midst of thine heart. For they are life unto those that find them, and health to all their flesh" (Prov. 4:21–22).

We read in Exodus 15:26, "I am the Lord that healeth thee." Jesus said, "And as Moses lifted up the serpent in the wilderness, even so must the Son of man be lifted up: That whosoever believeth in him should not perish, but have eternal life" (John 3:14–15).

Dear beloved, we see in receiving the words of Jesus, it brings not only life to our souls and spirits but to these physical bodies. For His words are medicine to our bodies through faith.

> *Jesus, You are the Great Physician. Anoint me with the oil of Your healing. Amen.*
>
> —FEBRUARY–MARCH 1907

Day 33

The Feast of Tabernacles

When ye have gathered in the fruit of the land, ye shall keep a feast unto the Lord seven days . . . and ye shall rejoice before the Lord your God seven days.

—LEVITICUS 23:39–40

THIS IS THE FEAST of the full harvest. In this you see a type of baptized, Holy-Ghost people filled with divine love, and under the mighty power of the Holy Spirit, praising God and giving Him the glory. Hallelujah!

This Feast of Tabernacles is a type of a continual feast with Jesus. It typifies the coming and reigning of our Lord and Savior, Jesus Christ, when He shall spread the tabernacle and feed us.

We are the tabernacle. His Spirit indwells us. Just as that original tabernacle was holy unto the Lord, so we too must be holy unto our Lord. "Know ye not that ye are the temple of God, and that the Spirit of God dwelleth in you? If any man defile the temple of God, him shall God destroy; for the temple of God is holy, which temple ye are" (1 Cor. 3:16–17).

These types and shadows represent what we are now receiving in reality. Bless His name. May we all seek all that God has for us.

> *Lord, sanctify me so that Your Spirit might tabernacle with me and be honored in my life. Amen.*
> —JUNE–SEPTEMBER 1907

Day 34

Who May Prophesy?

And it shall come to pass in the last days, saith God, I will pour out of my Spirit upon all flesh: and your sons and your daughters shall prophesy.

—ACTS 2:17

IT IS THE privilege of all the members of the bride of Christ to prophesy, which means testify or preach. Before Pentecost, the woman could only go into the "court of the women" and not into the inner court. The anointing oil was never poured on a woman's head but only on the heads of kings, prophets, and priests. But when our Lord poured out Pentecost, He brought all those faithful women with the other disciples into the upper room, and God baptized them all in the same room and made no difference. All the women received the anointed oil of the Holy Ghost and were able to preach the same as the men.

The woman is the weaker vessel and represents the tenderness of Christ, while the man represents the firmness of Christ. They both were co-workers in Eden and both fell into sin; so they both have to come together and work in the gospel (1 Cor. 11:11–12). No woman who has the Spirit of Jesus wants to usurp authority over the man.

It is contrary to the Scriptures that any woman should not have her part in the salvation work to which God has called her. We have no right to lay a straw in her way.

Remember Paul's teaching, "There is neither Jew nor Greek, there is neither bond nor free, there is neither male nor female: for ye are all one in Christ Jesus" (Gal. 3:28).

> *Spirit of God, pour out upon Your sons and daughters in our generation to prophesy in Jesus' name. Amen.*
> —JANUARY 1908

Day 35

Pure Channels

Draw nigh to God, and he will draw nigh to you. Cleanse your hands, ye sinners; and purify your hearts, ye double-minded.

—JAMES 4:8

IF MEN AND women today will consecrate themselves to God—their hands and feet and eyes and affections, body and soul, all sanctified—how the Holy Ghost will use such people.

He will find pure channels to flow through, sanctified avenues for His power. People will be saved, sanctified, healed, and baptized with the Holy Ghost and fire.

The baptism of the Holy Ghost comes through our Lord and Savior Jesus Christ by faith in His Word. In order to receive it, we must first be sanctified. Then we can become His witnesses unto the uttermost parts of the earth.

You will never have an experience to measure

with Acts 2:4 and Acts 2:16–17 until you get your personal Pentecost for the baptism with the Holy Ghost and fire (Matt. 3:11).

This is the latter rain that God is pouring out upon His humble children in the last days. We are preaching a gospel that measures with the great commission that Jesus gave His disciples when He arose from the dead (Matt. 28:19–20). They received the power to implement this commission on the day of Pentecost (Acts 2:4). Bless the Lord. Oh, how I bless God to see His mighty power manifested in these last days. God wants His people to receive the baptism with the Holy Ghost and fire.

Spirit, make of me a pure channel
through which You will flow. Amen.
—W. J. SEYMOUR
MAY 1908

Day 36

Laying On of Hands

For John truly baptized with water; but ye shall be baptized with the Holy Ghost not many days hence.

—ACTS 1:5

IT IS NOT necessary to have hands laid on you to receive the baptism of the Holy Ghost. You can receive the baptism in your closet. The gift of the Holy Ghost comes in response to faith in the Word of God. You may receive the Holy Ghost right now, that is if you are sanctified. Read Acts 1:5 and cry out to the Father through the Son, "Lord Jesus, baptize me with the Holy Ghost."

The baptism of the Spirit is a gift of power on the sanctified life. When people receive it, sooner or later they will speak in tongues as the Spirit gives utterance. A person may not speak in tongues for a week after the baptism, but as soon as he gets to praying or praising God in the liberty of the Spirit, the tongues will follow. Tongues are not salvation. It is a gift that God throws in with the baptism of the Holy Spirit. People do not have to travail and agonize for the baptism, for when our work ceases, then God comes. We cease from our own work, and God takes control.

Lord Jesus, baptize me with the Holy Spirit. Amen.

—JANUARY 1908

Day 37

Love

And now abideth faith, hope, charity, these three; but the greatest of these is charity.

—1 CORINTHIANS 13:13

IT IS SWEET to have the promise of Jesus and the character of Jesus wrought out in our lives and hearts by the power of the blood and the Holy Ghost, and to have that same love and that same meekness. Jesus was a man of love—the love of God incarnate in a body.

We must have that pure love that comes down from heaven. Such love is willing to suffer loss, not puffed up, not easily provoked, but gentle, meek, and humble. We are accounted as sheep for the slaughter day by day. We are crucified to self, the world, the flesh, and everything, that we may bear about in our body the dying of the Lord Jesus so that our joy may be full even as He is full.

Jesus, Author of Love, fill me with Your love and joy that I might love others. Amen.

—NOVEMBER 1906

Day 38

The Spirit Follows the Blood

*And such were some of you: but ye are
washed, but ye are sanctified, but ye are
justified in the name of the Lord Jesus,
and by the Spirit of our God.*

—1 CORINTHIANS 6:11

JESUS SAID, "Now ye are clean through the
word which I have spoken unto you"
(John 15:3). That cleansing took place before
the Pentecostal baptism. Jesus said on that
night before He was betrayed, "Ye are not all
clean" (John 13:11). Jesus knew that Judas had
the devil in him.

The disciples had been sanctified before
Pentecost, for the Word of God is true. We
know they had been justified a long time
before, for He said, "Rejoice not, that the
spirits are subject unto you; but rather rejoice,
because your names are written in heaven"
(Luke 10:20). And we know they were sanctified when Jesus prayed for them, for Jesus'
prayers did not have to be answered in the

future but were answered in the present. He said, "They are not of the world, even as I am not of the world" (John 17:16).

They were not only sanctified but had received the Holy Spirit in a certain measure, because He breathed on them in the upper room and said, "Receive ye the Holy Ghost" (John 20:22).

The heart must be clean before the Holy Ghost can endue with power from on high. It is not the work of the Holy Ghost to burn up inherited sin and carnality. He is not our Savior. It is the blood that cleanses us from all sin. The disciples were cleansed and sanctified and were sitting and waiting when the Holy Ghost fell upon them.

We know also that Cornelius was clean, for when the Lord let down the sheet before Peter. "What God hath cleansed, that call not thou common" (Acts 10:15).

Spirit of God, fall upon me as at Pentecost. Amen.

Day 39

The Way Into the Holiest

Let us draw near with a true heart in full assurance of faith, having our hearts sprinkled from an evil conscience, and our bodies washed with pure water.

—HEBREWS 10:22

A SINNER COMES to the Lord all wrapped up in sin and darkness. He cannot make any consecration because he is dead. The life has to be put into us before we can present any life to the Lord. He must get justified by faith. There is a Lamb without spot and blemish, slain before God for him. When the sinner repents toward God for his sins, the Lord has mercy on him for Christ's sake, and puts eternal life in his soul, pardoning him of his sins, washing away his guilty pollution, and he stands before God justified as if he had never sinned.

Then there remains that old original sin in him for which he is not responsible until he has the light. He hears that "Jesus also, that He might sanctify the people with his own blood, suffered without the gate" (Heb. 13:12). So he comes to be sanctified. There is Jesus, the Lamb without blemish, on the altar. Jesus takes that soul that has eternal life in it and presents it to God for thorough purging and cleansing from all sin.

Now he is on the altar ready for the fire of God to fall, which is the baptism with the Holy Ghost. It is a free gift upon the sanctified, cleansed heart. The fire remains there continually, burning in the holiness of God.

He stays there and the great Shekinah glory is continually burning and filling him with heavenly light.

Lord, keep me on the altar. Amen.
—W. J. SEYMOUR
OCTOBER 1906

Day 40

Sanctified Before Pentecost

*Now ye are clean through the word which
I [Jesus] have spoken unto you.*
—JOHN 15:3

BY READING the Bible carefully, you can see that the disciples were saved and sanctified men; and had received the unction of the Holy Spirit before the day of Pentecost.

In John 17:15–17, Jesus prays, "I pray not that thou shouldest take them out of the world, but that thou shouldest keep them from the evil. They are not of the world, even as I am not of the world. Sanctify them through thy truth: thy word is truth." Jesus is the word and the truth, so they were sanctified through the truth the very night that He prayed for them.

Jesus said to the disciples, "Peace be unto you: as my Father hath sent me, even so send I you. And when He had said this, He breathed on them and saith unto them 'Receive ye the Holy Ghost: Whosesoever sins ye remit, they are remitted unto them; and whose soever sins ye retain, they are retained'" (John 20:21–23).

The disciples were filled with the unction of the Holy Spirit—the anointing—before the day of Pentecost when Jesus breathed on them. This sustained them until they were endued with power from on high.

In the first chapter of Acts, Jesus taught His disciples to wait for the promise of the Father. This was not to wait for sanctification. His blood had been spilt on Calvary's cross. He was not going to send His blood to cleanse them from carnality, but His Spirit to endue them with power. They went up to Jerusalem praising and blessing God with great joy. They all continued with one accord in prayer and supplication.

Jesus, pour out Your Spirit on me, that Joel's prophecy might be fulfilled in my life. Amen.

—DECEMBER 1906

Day 41

Sanctification

For this is the will of God, even your sanctification. . . .

—1 THESSALONIANS 4:3

THERE IS NOTHING sweeter, higher, or holier in this world than sanctification. The baptism with the Holy Ghost is the gift of power upon the sanctified soul, giving power to preach the Gospel of Christ and power to go to the stake. It seals you unto the day of redemption, that you may be ready to meet the Lord Jesus at midnight or any time, because you have oil in your vessel with your lamp.

You are partaker of the Holy Ghost in the Pentecostal baptism, just as you were partaker of the Lord Jesus Christ in sanctification. You become partaker of the eternal Spirit of God in the baptism with the Holy Ghost.

Jesus was God's Son before He received the baptism, sanctification and was sent into the world, but yet He could not go on His great mission, fighting against the combined forces of hell, until He received the baptism with the Holy Ghost. If He needed it, how much more we as His servants ought to get the same thing.

Jesus, baptize me with Your Spirit that I might be empowered to serve You in all that I do. Amen.
—FEBRUARY–MARCH 1906

Day 42

Christ Abides in Sanctification

I will never leave thee, nor forsake thee.
—HEBREWS 13:5

WHEN WE receive Christ as our sanctifier, He comes in and we have the abiding anointing in our souls continually. When a man is sanctified, there is no doubt as to his sanctification, for he has the witness within. Christ abides. He sits enthroned. You are in the Word of God and you get a real witness from the throne of God that Christ is within you. When you call your Beloved, He answers and says, "Here am I."

I remember after I was converted, I said, "How is this? My beloved comes to me and visits me, but He does not abide." I knew I was a Christian but I did not have the real abiding anointing. When I would get with Christians and sing one or two hymns, my

Beloved would come and visit me. But when I left, it seemed He would go. I said to Him, "I would like for you to come and stay, not just come and fill me and afterwards take Your flight."

When I go to my Beloved, who is sanctified in me, He comes and makes my soul laugh. You do not have to ask someone about it. If you have not received the abiding anointing, you have counterfeit sanctification. As long as you live in the Word of God, He will always be present. We must continue to obey Him, for there is no way for Christ to abide in us, if we do not obey Him

> *Jesus, remain with me. Indwell me with Your Word. Sanctify me. Fill me with Your joy and laughter. Amen.*
> —JUNE–SEPTEMBER 1907

Day 43

We Cannot Afford It

*Submit yourselves therefore to God. Resist
the devil, and he will flee from you.*
—James 4:7

WE CANNOT AFFORD to sell Satan even a small piece of ground in our hearts. Because if we do, he will have right of way at the gate to get to it. The only way to keep Satan out is to live a holy Spirit-filled life in the Word.

Many people today have sold themselves for naught. They have sold a piece of the land which has been redeemed by the blood of Christ. They have sold land to Satan in order to commit adultery, to steal, to beat, or to cheat. But, praise our God, He has sent us the Word of God to uncover men's sins by the power of the Holy Ghost, that they may be loosed from these spirits of bondage.

If the enemy finds a weak place in us, he is

going to come in various ways to entice us to
sell him a piece of land, so he can sow his wild
oats in it. We should be like Jesus. When the
enemy tried to bargain with Him for the land
of the world, offering Jesus the whole world if
He would fall down and worship him, Jesus
would not bow. Satan had no power. He had
no right of way.

Never bow down or compromise at any
terms with the world, the flesh, or the devil.

*In Jesus' name, I resist Satan and bind
myself to God's Word in obedience to
His will and way for my life. Amen.*
—JANUARY 1908

Day 44

The Holy Ghost and the Bride

The Spirit and the bride say, Come.
—REVELATION 22:17

HOW SWEET IT IS for us to have this blessed privilege of being a coworker with the Holy Ghost. He inspires us with faith in God's Word and endues us with power for service for the Master.

Every man and woman who receives the baptism of the Holy Ghost is the bride of Christ. They have a missionary spirit for saving souls. They have the spirit of Pentecost. "And let him that heareth say, Come. And let him that is athirst come. And whosoever will, let him take the water of life freely" (Rev. 22:17).

The bride of Christ is calling the thirsty to come to Jesus because this is the work of the Holy Ghost in the believer. He intercedes for the lost. He groans for them. The Spirit also calls the believer to come to Jesus and get sanctified. He points the sanctified to Jesus for a baptism with the Holy Ghost.

Christ's bride is pure and spotless. "Thou art all fair, my love; there is no spot in thee." (Song of Sol. 4:7). Christ's bride is clean and free from sin and all impurity. He gave Himself for her, that He might sanctify and cleanse the church with the washing of water by the Word.

Christ's bride has but one husband (2 Cor. 11:2). She is subject to Him (Eph. 5:24). The Bridegroom is the Son of God (2 Cor. 11:2).

Not only when Christ comes are we married to Christ, but right now, if you are sanctified and baptized with the Holy Ghost and fire, you are married to Him already.

> *Jesus, satisfy my thirst for Your living water with Your Spirit. Overflow my desert with Your oasis of refreshing. Amen.*

—W. J. SEYMOUR
MAY 1908

Day 45

The Witness

He that believeth on the Son of God hath the witness in himself.

—1 JOHN 5:10

E BELIEVE in a real salvation that gives you the witness by the Spirit. Calvin taught a salvation that if you said you had it, you did not have it; and if you had it, you did not know it; and if you lost it, you could not get it again.

Wesley taught that if you had it you would know it, and if you lost it, you could get it again. The Bible confirms we have a witness to our salvation—the Spirit, the water, and the blood (1 John 5:8).

We teach that if a man is ensnared by the devil, and has not trampled the blood of Jesus Christ under his feet and counted the blood wherewith he was sanctified a holy thing, he can get back to Jesus Christ by restitution, faith, and by doing his first works over.

> *Lord Jesus, bear witness in me with*
> *the blood, baptism, and Spirit of my*
> *salvation in You. Amen.*
>
> —SEPTEMBER 1907

Day 46

Crucified With Christ

I am crucified with Christ: nevertheless I live; yet not I, but Christ liveth in me: and the life which I now live in the flesh I live by the faith of the Son of God.
—GALATIANS 2:20

JESUS IS SEARCHING for a people who will believe the gospel. He has never changed the gospel in any way since He commissioned it. Many take sanctification to be the power. They stop when they have the original sin taken out and Christ has been enthroned on their hearts. But God wants us to go on to be filled with the Holy Ghost that we may be witnesses unto Him to the uttermost parts of the earth.

The times of ignorance God winked at, but now He commands men everywhere to repent. The Lord is restoring all the gifts to His church. He wants people everywhere to repent. He wants a people who have faith in His Word and in the Holy Spirit.

Jesus was not only nailed to the cross, but hung there until He died. He did not come down from the cross as they told Him to do, though He had the power to do so. So with us, when we are crucified with Christ, we should not come down and live for self again, but stay on the cross. A constant death to self is the way to follow our Master.

Lord, I desire to be crucified to self so that I may live totally for You. Amen.

—OCTOBER 1906

Day 47

The Promise Is Still Good

For John truly baptized with water; but
ye shall be baptized with the Holy Ghost
not many days hence.

—ACTS 1:5

ONE HUNDRED TWENTY faithful believers on the day of Pentecost were baptized with the Holy Ghost according to promise. The converts of Philip in the Samaritan revival were baptized with the Holy Ghost when Peter and John came from Jerusalem and preached the doctrine to them. The household of Cornelius received the same endowment of power, showing that the promise was also extended to the Gentiles.

Again to the Corinthian church is the record given of the fulfillment of the promise. That the apostolic church had wonderful power is evidenced by its remarkable growth, as well as by the record of the Word.

But didn't Paul prophesy that these things

should be done away? We have only to read 1 Corinthians 13:9–10 to be set clear. "For we know in part, and we prophesy in part. But when that which is perfect is come, then that which is in part shall be done away."

Paul knew only in part, prophesied in part, and spoke in tongues only in part. But when that which is perfect is come, then the knowledge, prophecy, and tongues of Paul shall be done away. If they are to be done away on that great and notable day of the Lord, so they must be in existence when He shall come. Divine love never fails.

Spirit of God, baptize me according to the Word that I might know the power of Your promise. Amen.

—SEPTEMBER 1906

Day 48

Spread the Fire

*For by one Spirit are we all baptized into
one body, whether we be Jews or Gentiles,
whether we be bond or free; and have
been all made to drink into one Spirit.*

—1 CORINTHIANS 12:13

WHEN BROTHER William Pendleton and
thirty-five of his members were turned
out of the Holiness church, they were invited by
Brother Bartleman and other workers to
occupy the church at Eighth Street and Maple
Avenue. It had just been opened up for
Pentecostal work. And God has been using
them as never before.

When some of the saints were rejected from
the Nazarene church at Elysian Heights on
account of the baptism with the Holy Ghost and
evidence of tongues, they opened cottage
prayer meetings where hungry souls flocked.

"Truth crushed to earth will rise again.
The eternal years of God are hers;

But error wounded writhes in pain,
And dies among its worshipers."

In California where there has been no unity
among churches, they are becoming one
against this Pentecostal movement. But, thank
God, the source is from the skies and cannot
be cut off from below. The dear church people
know not what they do. Many of them are
hungry and coming and saying, "This is just
what I have been longing for, for years."

God is drawing His people together and
making them one. No new church or division
of the body of Christ is being formed. Christ
never had but one church. We may be turned
out of the big wood and brick structures, but
"By one Spirit are we all baptized into one
body" (1 Cor. 12:13).

> *Lord God, make us one as the Father*
> *and the Son are one, that we might*
> *dwell in the unity of the Spirit. Amen.*
> —OCTOBER 1906

Day 49

The True Pentecost

Greater is he that prophesieth than he that speaketh with tongues.

—1 CORINTHIANS 14:5

WE CAN HAVE ALL the nine gifts as well as the nine fruits of the Spirit, for in Christ Jesus dwells all the fullness of the Godhead bodily. Paul is simply teaching the church to be in unity and not to be confused because all have not the same gifts.

We are not confused because one has his Pentecost and another has not been sanctified. We do not say that we do not need the justified or the sanctified brother simply because he does not speak with tongues or does not prophesy. But we realize that it takes the justified, the sanctified and the Pentecost brother all to make up the body of Christ.

You may have the gift of wisdom, healing, or prophecy, but when you get the Pentecost, the Lord God will speak through you in tongues.

"Greater is he that prophesieth than he that speaketh with tongues, except he interpret." The brother that prophesies is no greater than the brother that speaks in tongues if the brother interprets as he speaks. We have a good many here that interpret as they speak, and it is edifying. The gifts are for you if you will only ask the Lord for them.

In 1 Corinthians 14, Paul is setting us in order that have the baptism with the Holy Ghost and the speaking in tongues, that we should not get puffed up. In getting into deep spiritual things and into the hidden mysteries of God, people have to keep very humble at the feet of the Lord Jesus, for these precious gifts can easily puff us up, if we do not keep under the blood.

Jesus, I seek You above the gifts. Give me those gifts You desire that I may minister Your grace to others. Amen.

—December 1906

Preserved and Sealed

Now he which stablisheth us with you in Christ, and hath anointed us, is God; Who hath also sealed us, and given the earnest of the Spirit in our hearts.
—2 CORINTHIANS 1:21–22

THE BLOOD OF Jesus Christ sweetens a person. We cannot have much confidence in a religion that does not keep a person sweet. If there is jealousy or any of the works of the flesh manifest, the devil must have slipped in. This salvation sweetens, seasons, and preserves you. To preserve a thing means to keep it. In order to preserve milk, you must wash the vessel and sometimes sun it. Then it is fit to fill with the sweet milk, and when you want a drink you go into the pantry and pour it out, and oh, how good it is.

So the Lord cleanses the vessels and makes them sweet and pure. Then He fills them with His holy love that keeps them saved and sanctified. He could not put it into a dirty vessel.

The Lord has cleansed vessels, and your soul is the vessel. He cleanses from all unrighteousness and afterward pours in oil. And when He fills you up with oil, then He sends you out to proclaim His precious Word. This oil keeps us pure and sweet and preserved. He also seals you with the Holy Spirit of God unto the day of Redemption (Eph. 4:30). He seals you to keep anything from getting in that would sour or embitter. When we obey the Word of God, no sin can enter, for the blood preserves us, and Christ is enthroned within.

The devil is on the outside. Christ sways His scepter of righteousness and true holiness, and keeps the place clean.

> *Purify me, Oh, Lord. Cleanse me with Your blood. Seal me with Your Spirit unto the day of my redemption. Amen.*

—February–March 1906

Day 51

Cured of Doubt and Fear

For God hath not given us the spirit of fear; but of power, and of love, and of a sound mind.

—2 Timothy 1:7

THE BLOOD OF Jesus is the only cure for doubt and fear. It takes sanctification to deliver a person from doubts and fear. We always find that people who are not sanctified are more or less troubled with doubt. But when they get sanctified they are filled with such love to God, that they are like little babes, they believe every word of Jesus.

Jesus had been with the disciples three and a half years, and had told them all about the kingdom, and yet the doubts and fears came upon them. But in Luke 24:31 we read, "And their eyes were opened, and they knew Him." After the resurrection their spiritual eyes were opened to know Jesus.

Our eyes must be opened to see our

inheritance. No one can get the baptism until Christ anoints his eyes and opens up his understanding that he might understand the Scriptures. "Then opened He their understanding, that they might understand the scriptures" (Luke 24:45). Then they received the living Word into their hearts, and their hearts burned within them as He unfolded the Scriptures to them.

Sanctification is a cure for unbelief, doubts, and fears. Jesus got all His disciples cured before He went back to glory. What do you call that but sanctification?

We can see that Jesus taught the doctrine of sanctification before He was crucified, for He had prayed that they might be sanctified in John 17. He stayed with them on earth forty days, opened their understanding, opened their eyes, and cleansed them of doubt.

> *Jesus, empower me to conquer the spirit of fear and timidity that I might walk in bold faith. Amen.*
> —JUNE–SEPTEMBER 1907

Day 52

Those With a Harsh Spirit

Howbeit when he, the Spirit of truth, is come, he will guide you into all truth: for he shall not speak of himself.

—JOHN 16:13

THE CHARACTER and work of the Holy Ghost is love. If you find someone with a harsh spirit, and that person even talks in tongues in a harsh spirit, it is not the Holy Ghost talking. His utterances are in power, glory, and with blessing and sweetness.

The character of the Holy Ghost is precisely like Jesus, the Word of truth, for the Holy Ghost is "the spirit of truth." He speaks always of the Word and makes everything like the Word. Jesus was the Son of God, the suffering Christ.

The Holy Ghost comes into the world to reveal this suffering Christ to us. He is a meek and humble Spirit—not a harsh Spirit. He is a Spirit of glory.

When the Spirit comes into believers, He comes to tell them all about Jesus' salvation. He reveals Christ. He paints Him as the wonderful Son of God, the brightest gem the Father had in heaven—our only hope of salvation and reconciliation with the Father. How sweet it is to have the Holy Ghost come to you and show you Jesus through the Word. He witnesses and reveals through the Word, and never gets outside of the Word.

Speak through me, Holy Spirit, with a tongue of praise for Jesus, and still all criticism and harsh talk. Amen.

—MAY 1908

Day 53

Pray Through

The effectual fervent prayer of a righteous man availeth much.

—JAMES 5:16

W E OUGHT NOT to stop until we pray through and receive our requests from God. We should prevail with God until we get a witness. Elijah prayed for rain and sent his servant seven times until he got the witness, which was a cloud the size of a man's hand. Then Elijah arose and went to tell Ahab that the rain was coming (1 Kings 18:42–44).

Paul prayed thrice for a certain thing before God answered him (2 Cor. 12:8). God heard the first time, but Paul did not get the answer until he had prayed three times.

Oh, we should press or claim before the throne until we receive a witness by the power of the Holy Ghost. God will do just what He promises.

*Lord, I will pray through my need to
Your will. Amen.*

—MAY 1908

Day 54

Traditions and Dead Forms

Making the word of God of none effect through your tradition, which ye have delivered: and many such like things do ye.
—MARK 7:13

OH, IT IS EASY to follow the Spirit of God if you have been born of the Spirit. And it is easy to manifest the Spirit if the Spirit of God is within you. It is impossible for both good and impure water to come from the same spring. Just as surely as the blood of Jesus Christ has been applied to the soul, you will not only know it, but your neighbors will know it. And those working with you will know it.

It means so much to have the blood of Jesus Christ applied to your soul. Dead forms and ceremonies are done away and every sin must be washed away by the blood of Jesus.

It is not tomorrow *in* sin and today *out* of sin, but if the blood of Jesus has atoned for

you, it has atoned for *today* and *tomorrow*—
once and for all.

> *Lord, crucify my old forms, traditions,*
> *and ceremonies which keep me from*
> *walking daily in the Spirit. Amen.*
> —SEPTEMBER 1907

Day 55

United With Jesus

Take my yoke upon you, and learn of me.
—MATTHEW 11:29

THE LORD HAS shown us that this yoke was the covenant of the New Testament in His blood. We put this yoke on when we are baptized with the Holy Ghost. This covenant is like marriage. We are married, not for one day or year or even life. We are married for eternity. When I get married to Jesus Christ, taking His yoke upon me, we are in covenant for eternal life. Jesus and I are united.

> *Jesus, thank You for loving me so much that You put upon me Your yoke of love forever. Amen.*

—OCTOBER 1906

Day 56

God's Fire Is Still Falling

*I [John] indeed baptize you with water
unto repentance: but he that cometh after
me is mightier than I . . . he shall baptize
you with the Holy Ghost and with fire.*
—MATTHEW 3:11

THE WAVES OF Pentecostal salvation are
still rolling in at Azusa Street Mission.
From morning until late at night the meetings
continue, usually with three altar services a
day. We have kept no record of souls saved,
sanctified, and baptized with the Holy Ghost,
but a brother said last week he counted about
fifty in all that had been baptized with the
Holy Ghost during the week. Then at Eighth
Street and Map Avenue, the People's Church,
Monrovia, Whittier, Hermon, Sawtelle,
Pasadena, Elysian Heights, and other places
the work is going on and souls are coming
through amid great rejoicing.

Four of the Holiness preachers have
received the baptism with the Holy Ghost.

One of them, Brother William Pendleton, with his congregation being turned out of the church, is holding meetings at Eighth Street and Maple Avenue. There is a heavenly atmosphere there. The altar is filled with seekers. People are slain under the power of God and are rising up in a life baptized with the Holy Ghost.

The fire is spreading. People are writing from different points to know about this Pentecost, and are beginning to wait on God.

He is no respecter of persons and places. We expect to see a wave of salvation go over this world. While this work has been going on for five years, it has burst out in great power on this coast. There is power in the full gospel. Nothing can quench it.

> *Jesus, baptize me with Your fire that I might be consumed with passion for You. Amen.*

—OCTOBER 1906

Day 57

Brother Pendleton's Testimony

And we know that all things work together for good to them that love God, to them who are the called according to his purpose.

—ROMANS 8:28

WHEN MY PLACE of worship was taken away from me, I said, "Lord, I trusted you once, and you gave me a better place." And praise God, He gave me the best place I ever had in my life and gave me more people to listen to the gospel than I ever had before. God will never allow things to be taken from us but that He will give us better than ever before.

There is not a veil or shadow between heaven and my soul today. I am getting more from God than ever in my life. My prospects of heaven are getting stronger and stronger. There is no life that gives a man such an assurance of heaven as the life in the baptism with the Holy Ghost and fire. God the Father, God the Son, and God the Holy Ghost can use these members to His own glory.

> *Lord, help me to endure temporary setbacks in order to see Your eternal purposes accomplished. I believe that in Your grace the best is yet to come. Amen.*

—OCTOBER 1906

Day 58

The Sin Against the Holy Ghost

He that shall blaspheme against the Holy Ghost hath never forgiveness, but is in danger of eternal damnation: because they said, He hath an unclean spirit.

—MARK 3:29–30

THE SIN AGAINST the Holy Ghost cannot be forgiven. People who have a real knowledge of the Holy Ghost in their hearts by the Holy Spirit, and then say this work is of the devil or people are speaking in tongues by the devil, after they have the knowledge of the truth, such people are in danger of sinning against the Holy Ghost.

"And whosoever shall speak a word against the Son of man, it shall be forgiven him: but unto him that blasphemeth against the Holy Ghost it shall not be forgiven" (Luke 12:10).

When men sin against the Son, they are forgiven, but when they sin against God the Father, God the Son, and God the Holy Ghost, they have sinned against them all, so there is no more forgiveness. There is no fourth person to do any interceding for them.

People have not sinned against the Holy Ghost unless they have willfully denied the blood of Jesus Christ and trampled it under their feet (Heb. 10:26). Some have been ensnared by the enemy and have lost the Pentecost and lost sanctification and lost justification. It has brought sadness, and they can repent because they did not do it willfully. They were overpowered by the enemy, and not understanding, they yielded to it.

> *Jesus, guide and direct me that I may never sin against Your precious Holy Spirit. Amen.*

—DECEMBER 1906

Day 59

A Type of Pentecost

Wherefore all the men of Israel assembled themselves unto the king in the feast which was in the seventh month.

—2 Chronicles 5:3

A BEAUTIFUL PICTURE of Pentecost is seen in this precious Word of God from 2 Chronicles. That feast was a type of Pentecost. And all the men of Israel came and they brought up the ark of the tabernacle of the congregation and all the holy vessels that were in the tabernacle. All of this was a type of our consecration and sanctification unto the Lord.

"It came even to pass, as the trumpeters and singers were as one, to make one sound to be heard in praising and thanking the Lord; and when they lifted up their voice with the trumpets and cymbals and instruments of music, and praised the Lord, saying, 'For he is good; for his mercy endureth forever:' that then the house was filled with a cloud, even the house of the Lord; so that the priests could not stand to minister by reason of the cloud: for the glory of the Lord had filled the house of God" (2 Chron. 5:13–14).

The Levites, which were the singers, were arrayed in white linen. Linen is a type of the robes of righteousness that we read of in Revelation 7:13–14, "And one of the elders answered, saying unto me, 'What are these which are arrayed in white robes? and whence came they? And I said unto him, Sir, thou knowest. And he said to me, These are they which came out of great tribulation, and have washed their robes, and made them white in the blood of the Lamb."

And when they praised the Lord in unison, the house was filled with the glory of the Lord.

> *Lord, how I desire to be filled with Your Spirit and to be in the glory of Your presence! Amen.*

—APRIL 1907

𝔅𝔦𝔰𝔥𝔬𝔭 𝔬𝔣 𝔱𝔥𝔢 ℭ𝔥𝔲𝔯𝔠𝔥

And I will pray the Father, and he shall give you another Comforter, that he may abide with you for ever.

—JOHN 14:16

IT IS THE OFFICE of the Holy Spirit to preside over the entire work of God on earth. Jesus was our Bishop while on earth, but now He has sent the Holy Ghost to take His place, not men (John 14:16, 15:26, 16:7–14).

The Holy Ghost infuses us with divine power and invests us with heavenly authority. No religious assembly is legal without His presence and His transaction. We should recognize Him as the Teacher of teachers.

Many people today think we need new church buildings, stone structures, brick structures, modern improvements, new choirs, and trained singers right from the conservatories. Some believe in paying large sums of money for singing, fine pews, fine chandeliers, everything that could attract the human heart in order to win souls to the meeting house that is used in this twentieth century.

The church had the right idea that we need bishops and elders, but they must be given authority by our Lord and Savior Jesus Christ. Their qualifications for these offices must be the enduement of the power of the Holy Ghost. Jesus said, "Ye have not chosen me, but I have chosen you, and ordained you, that ye should go and bring forth fruit, and that your fruit should remain: that whatsoever ye shall ask of the Father in my name, he may give it you" (John 15:16). Praise our God!

> *Lord, what we need to revive our churches is not more stuff, but more of You. Amen.*

—W. J. SEYMOUR
JUNE–SEPTEMBER 1907

Sanctified by the Cross

*I pray not that thou shouldest take them
out of the world, but that thou shouldest
keep them from the evil. . . . Sanctify
them through thy truth: thy word is truth.*
—JOHN 17:15, 17

JESUS IS STILL praying this prayer today for
every believer to come and be sanctified.
Sanctification makes us one with the Lord
Jesus (Heb. 2:11). Sanctification makes us
holy as Jesus is holy.

Paul writes in 1 Thessalonians 4:3, "For this
is the will of God, even your sanctification."
So it is His will for every soul to be saved from
all sin, actual and original. Actual sins are
those we willfully commit, while original sin is
that which we inherited from the first Adam.
All sin is cleansed away through the blood of
Jesus Christ. We must die to the old man.
"Knowing this, that our old man is crucified
with him, that the body of sin might be
destroyed, that henceforth we should not serve

sin. For he that is dead is freed from sin" (Rom. 6:6).

God is calling His people to true holiness in these days. We thank God for the blessed light that He is giving us. "If a man therefore purge himself from these, he shall be a vessel unto honour, sanctified, and meet for the master's use" (2 Tim. 2:21). He means for us to be purged from uncleanness and all kinds of sin. Sanctification makes us holy and destroys the breed of sin, the love of sin, and carnality. It makes us pure and whiter than snow.

> *Sanctify me, Lord, with Your Spirit*
> *that I may be cleansed by Your blood*
> *and empowered to do Your bidding.*
> *Amen.*

—W. J. SEYMOUR
MAY 1908

Day 62

Faith and Prayer

And all things, whatsoever ye shall ask in
prayer, believing, ye shall receive.
—Matthew 21:22

THE LORD wants us to have more faith.
When several are praying together for the
same petition and one has prayed the prayer of
faith, then the Holy Ghost will glorify Jesus by
witnessing that the prayer is heard.

But often someone will continue praying,
just as they did for Peter after God had brought
him out of the prison, and he was knocking at
the gate. Yet, they would not believe that
prayer could be so quickly answered.

If you continue to pray after receiving the
witness of the Holy Ghost, you grieve the
Spirit by doubting, and you show that you
barely trust Him. The Lord wants us to know
that He has heard us. We need to thank and
praise Him for answering and that will help us

a great deal when we pray. He does not want us to pray in doubt but in faith.

Lord, in faith I seek Your response. Amen.

—MAY 1908

Day 63

Healing

I am the Lord that healeth thee.
—EXODUS 15:26

SICKNESS AND DISEASE are destroyed through the precious atonement of Jesus. Oh, how we ought to honor the stripes of Jesus (Isa. 53). How we ought to honor that precious body which the Father sanctified and sent into the world, not simply set apart, but really sanctified—soul, body, and spirit. We have been set free from sickness, disease, and everything of the devil. Jesus' body, which knew no sin and disease, was given for these imperfect bodies of ours.

Not only is the atonement for the sanctification of our souls, but for the sanctification of our bodies from disease which was inherited from Adam. Every drop of blood we received from our mother was impure. Sickness is born in a child, just as original sin is born in the child. Jesus was manifested to destroy the works of the devil (1 John 3:8). Every sickness is of the devil.

Thank God we have a living Christ among us to heal our diseases. He will heal in every case. Now if Jesus bore our sicknesses, why should we bear them? So we receive full salvation and healing through the atonement of Jesus.

> *Jesus, by Your stripes I am healed.*
> *Empower me to believe, claim, walk*
> *in, and trust Your healing for every*
> *area of my life. Amen.*

—SEPTEMBER 1907

Day 64

Victory Follows Crucifixion

Nay, in all these things we are more than conquerors through him that loved us.
—ROMANS 8:37

THINK OF WHAT hung on that momentous hour that Jesus suffered. No hour in all history has been fraught with such eternal interests. It was a crucial hour and he was a willing offering. He said, "What shall I say? Father, save me from this hour: but for this cause came I unto this hour" (John 12:27).

There is a crucial hour in every man and woman's life. Someone now may be facing their cross, their Gethsemane. Will you say, "Father, save me from this hour?"

You know the blessing that came when Jesus endured the cross, despising the shame. Face the hour of opportunity. Some are drawing back. God will give you grace for the hour of your opportunity. Let us pray, "Lord save me from drawing back."

Our Christ, who went every step of the way, says, "I will never leave you or forsake you." When we get on the resurrection side of the cross, the glory and victory will be unspeakable.

> *Lord Jesus, save me from drawing back. Give me the strength to die to self that I might live for You. Amen.*
> —SEPTEMBER 1906

Day 65

The Elder Brother

And he was angry and would not go in. . . .

—LUKE 15:28

THE PRODIGAL SON had returned amid great rejoicing to his father's house. There was music and dancing, and perhaps the whole neighborhood was stirred up and came out to see what was happening. "There is joy in the presence of the angels of God over one sinner that repenteth" (Luke 15:10).

Father has certainly opened up His house on Azusa Street for the return of the prodigals. And they are coming in from the north, south, east, and west. The fatted calf is being killed daily, and the fine new garments of praise and salvation are being handed out to the poor prodigals who are so lean and weary, and covered with filth and rags.

There was one discordant voice in the

parable as told by Jesus. It was the elder brother. He is here also. The father called him "son," and he was "in the field." We do not read, however, that he was doing any work. It simply states that he was in the field.

If he had been hard at work all day plowing with a deep plow, with his father's interests at heart, would he not have rejoiced with the household at his brother's return?

Yes, the elder brother is angry and will not come in to the feast. He sits on the fence and finds fault, saying that the "new tongues" and other gifts that Father is handing out to His children are of the devil. The Father has gone out to him several times, and continues to entreat him to come in.

We are praying that the older brother will soften his heart and come in before it is too late.

Lord, remove any attitude from my heart that reflects the older brother. Amen.

—OCTOBER 1906

Day 66

Pruning and Purging

I am the true vine, and my Father is the husbandman. Every branch in me that beareth not fruit he taketh away.
—JOHN 15:1–2

LET ME WARN YOU, dear ones, don't try to prune one another. Let Jesus do the pruning and purging. If you see a brother or sister doing anything you do not approve of, instead of blazing it abroad, get down on your knees and say: "My Father, I honor You to bring them out of this fault."

Multitudes of Christians have gone to the wall for that very same thing. They tried to prune one another, tried to make others believe just as they believed, and think just as they thought. If this movement stands for anything, it stands for unity of mind. It was raised up to answer the prayer of Jesus, "That they all may be one; as thou, Father, art in me, and I in thee" (John 17:21).

What is the matter with the world today?

Here is a little selfish sect, and there is a denomination by itself. They do not love one another as God would have them. Let us honor every bit of God there is in one another. Let us honor the Holy Ghost to teach men to get them out of their error. Dear ones, watch and pray that ye enter not into temptation. Watch that something does not come in to grieve the Holy Spirit.

I pray, Oh, God, to give complete liberty to Your Spirit. Amen.

—MRS. ANNA HALL
OCTOBER 1906

Day 67

Beginning of Worldwide Revival

I dwell in the high and holy place, with
him also that is of a contrite and humble
spirit, to revive the spirit of the humble,
and to revive the heart of the contrite ones.
—ISAIAH 57:15

E ARE EXPECTING wonderful things from
the Lord for 1907. It is a jubilee year.
May we all spend it at His feet, learning of
Him. The closing up of the old year and
beginning of the new found us on our knees at
Azusa Mission. And as the new year was
announced, such a wave of glory, divine love,
and unity came over us. The meeting went on
all the next day.

The Lord did great things in 1906. Pentecost
first fell in Los Angeles on April 9. Since then
the good tidings have spread in two hemi-
spheres. Many are rejoicing in pardon, purity,
and the power of the Holy Ghost. Wherever
the work goes, souls are saved, and not only
saved from hell, but through and through and

prepared to meet the Lord at His coming.

They are being filled with the holy oil, the baptism with the Holy Ghost, and wherever they go, it is being poured out.

From the little mustard-seed faith that was given to a little company of people waiting on God in a cottage prayer meeting, a great tree has grown, so that people from all parts of the country are coming like birds to lodge in the branches thereof (Matt. 13:31–32). The faith is still growing, and we are still just in the beginning, earnestly contending for the faith once delivered unto the saints.

> *Lord, keep the unity of the Spirit among us as believers so that Your work of Pentecost might pour out on all flesh. Amen.*

—JANUARY 1907

Day 68

Is This of God?

Wherefore tongues are for a sign, not to them that believe, but to them that believe not.

—1 CORINTHIANS 14:22

IN THE SPRING and summer of 1906, God began to answer the very prolonged cry of some of His hungry children, a cry for a Pentecost with scripture evidence.

One after another became at last conscious, as the mighty power of God came upon them, that they were speaking in divine ecstasy with a voice that was not their own, and in a language whether of men and angels they knew not, for until some received the gift of interpretation it was not known what they said. They were speaking mysteries to God for their own strengthening (1 Cor. 14:3–4).

The work which the writer [from England] believes was of God then came nearer to us. He himself has heard (this year, 1907) numbers of Spirit-filled men and women and even children magnifying God in tongues. They were all trusting in the work of the cross, adoring the Crucified, and sinners were being converted. He was in eight meetings, and he praises God with full heart for that fellowship. He can witness that all are strengthened by the knowledge that the Holy Ghost has come into fuller possession. They are filled with joy unspeakable and full of glory (1 Pet. 1:7–8). But God is now graciously working in our midst with the signs and gifts.

The writer can testify as a rejoicing witness. He could write of very strange things. Earnest prayer has ascended for months and has been gloriously answered, and greater things are yet to happen. God is girding the whole world with this sign of His outpouring of the Spirit.

> *Pour over me, Oh, Spirit of God, that*
> *I might speak, sing, worship, and pray*
> *completely empowered by You. Amen.*
>
> —MAY 1907

Day 69

The Church

And hath put all things under his feet, and gave him to be the head over all things to the church, which is his body, the fulness of him that filleth all in all.
—EPHESIANS 1:22–23

E MUST ALWAYS recognize that a meeting house is simply a place where Christ's people gather to worship. A meeting house is not the church. The church is planted in our hearts, through the blood of Jesus Christ, for Christ said in Matthew 16:18, "Upon this rock I will build my church; and the gates of hell shall not prevail against it."

The first thing in every assembly is to see that He, the Holy Ghost, is installed as the Chairman. The reason why we have so many dried up missions and churches today is because they have not the Holy Ghost as the Chairman. They have some man in His place. Man is all right in his place—when he is filled with the power of the Holy Ghost. For it is not man who does the work, but the Holy Ghost sent by Jesus to work through this tabernacle of clay.

Jesus Christ is the Archbishop of these assemblies, and He must be recognized. When the members of His body commence sinning, the Holy Ghost, the Chairman and Bishop, the presiding Elder, convicts them. They don't have to go and ask their pastor or their preacher, for they feel conviction within their own souls that the glory has left them—the joy, peace, rest, and comfort. When they feel the lack in their souls, if they will confess their sins, then God, the Holy Ghost, will accept them back into the church.

> *Spirit of God, like a mighty river, flow*
> *out of Christ's church into the lives of*
> *others. Refresh and revive the church so*
> *that we may be a vessel of Your refreshing*
> *and revival in the lives of others. Amen.*
> —W. J. SEYMOUR
> JUNE–SEPTEMBER 1907

Day 70

Ministers—Flames of Fire

And let all the angels of God worship him. And of the angels he saith, Who maketh his angels spirits, and his ministers a flame of fire.

—HEBREWS 1:6–7

GOD'S MINISTERS are "a flame of fire." He wants all men and women on fire. He wants us not only saved from sin but on fire. The Holy Ghost is dynamite and fire in your soul. He wants us to have not only the thunder but the lightning. The Holy Ghost is lightning. He strikes men down with conviction, slays, and makes them come alive.

I put everything on the altar—all I had hoped and longed for I gave to the Lord. Then when I prayed, the fire came down and God sanctified me and made me holy. Then I went home and said, "I have another religion." Well, it was not another religion, but the old Ishmael was cast out and the carnal nature was destroyed. God filled me with love and then

closed the door and left me in that state.
Nothing could come in but love.

> *Lord, I come as a living sacrifice,*
> *putting all that I am and have on the*
> *altar to be consumed by the fire of*
> *Your love. Amen.*

—MAY 1908

Day 71

Pray in the Spirit

But ye, beloved, building up yourselves on your most holy faith, praying in the Holy Ghost. . . .

—JUDE 20

IF YOU PRAY in the Spirit, you will strike the spring of living water and it will bubble up in you. You will never get tired of praying because you pray in the Spirit.

You will have joy in your soul as you pray. But some pray and have no joy. They keep begging God without praise and rejoicing. When you almost pray through, do not stop.

Lord, I stand on Your Word and faithfulness that Your covenant promises will be fulfilled in my life. Amen.

—MAY 1908

Day 72

Jesus Is Coming

But as the days of Noah were, so shall also the coming of the Son of man be.
—MATTHEW 24:37

W HEN THE FLOOD came, the ark rose on the bosom of water. In this is a beautiful type of the coming of Jesus. Just as when the flood arose, the people of God were lifted by the ark toward the sky, so when Jesus Christ, who is our Ark, shall appear, we shall also appear with Him in glory.

Then as the ark came back and rested on Mount Ararat, so when the Lord Jesus comes back, we shall stand with Him on Mount Olive.

Christ comes and gets His saints before the great tribulation, which corresponds to the flood. The Word says that as it was in the days of Noah, so shall it be in the days of the coming of the Son of man. We see the same conditions now that prevailed then, so we know the time draws near.

The time has come when we must separate ourselves from this old world. Everything must be second to Jesus. Your treasure is in heaven. You are walking down here on earth, and winning souls, to pass the time until Jesus comes.

Come quickly, Lord Jesus! Amen.
—JANUARY 1908

Day 73

Tongues Convict Sinners

*Behold, are not all these which speak
Galileans? And how hear we every man
in our own tongue, wherein we were born?*
—ACTS 2:7–8

THE POWER of the Holy Spirit was greatly
manifested in our meetings by the
speaking in unknown tongues. This was much
criticized by the town and vicinity, so the prin-
cipal physician, who was familiar with several
different languages, was prevailed upon to go
to the meetings in order to denounce them as
a fake. Miss Tuthill, in an unknown language
to herself but known to the doctor as Italian,
spoke his full name, which no one in the town
knew save himself, telling him things that had
happened in his life twenty years ago, and on
up to the present time, until he cried for mercy
and fell on his knees seeking God.

He found full salvation the next day, and is
now a believer in the gospel that Jesus taught,

and also in the power of the Holy Ghost that was given unto us to witness to a living Christ. That physician now says he would rather pray for the sick than give drugs, and is seriously thinking of leaving his profession and going into the Lord's work.

Many precious souls have been saved, sanctified, and baptized with the Holy Ghost as a result of the preached Word under the Spirit's anointing.

> *Spirit of God, speak to my heart that*
> *I may be convicted of sin and set free*
> *to serve You totally. Amen.*

—CHARLES PARHAM
SEPTEMBER 1906

Day 74

Pentecost in Danville

But ye shall receive power, after that the
Holy Ghost is come upon you: and ye
shall be witnesses unto me. . . .

—ACTS 1:8

EAR SAINTS in Los Angeles: God be praised
for His power and grace. When we came
here from Los Angeles, we found that most of
the band to whom we had preached while here
before were backslidden and fussing among
themselves. But when they saw that God had
really done something wonderful for us, they
all came in and began to seek the Lord. Most
of them have been reclaimed, and quite a
number have been baptized with the Holy
Ghost and have received the foreign tongue.

One young girl received the baptism Friday
night, and she spoke in German. God sent us
a German to interpret. He said he could
understand everything perfectly. Sister Jennie
Evans has also received the German language,

and speaks it very fluently. Sister Garr improves every day in her Tibetan and Chinese. Oh, how I praise God that He ever gave us this wonderful experience of the baptism with the Holy Ghost.

The sick are being healed. Several have been healed. But, best of all, many are getting the light, and as the Bible opens to us, we rejoice for the precious truths that have been hidden from us for so long by the "tradition of the elders" (Mark 7:5). This is the greatest power I ever saw. Glory to God!

> *Lord, open my eyes that I may know You and the power of Your Holy Spirit. Amen.*

—A. G. GARR AND WIFE
OCTOBER 1906

Day 75

Rivers of Living Water

He that believeth on me, as the scripture hath said, out of his belly shall flow rivers of living water.

—JOHN 7:38

IN THE FOURTH chapter of John, the words come, "Jesus answered and said unto her, If thou knewest the gift of God, and who it is that saith to thee, Give me to drink; thou wouldest have asked of him, and he would have given thee living water" (John 4:10). Praise God for the living waters today that flow freely, for they come from God to every hungry and thirsty heart.

We are able to go in the mighty name of Jesus to the ends of the earth and water dry places, deserts, and solitary places, until these parched, sad, lonely hearts are made to rejoice in the God of their salvation. We want the rivers today.

In Jesus Christ we receive forgiveness of

sins, sanctification of our spirit, soul, and body, and upon sanctification we may receive the gift of the Holy Ghost that Jesus promised to His disciples, the promise of the Father. All this we get through the atonement. Hallelujah!

The prophet said that Jesus had borne our griefs and carried our sorrows. "He was wounded for our transgressions, bruised for our iniquities, the chastisement of our peace was upon him, and with his stripes we are healed" (Isa. 53:5). We have healing, health, salvation, joy, life—everything in Jesus. Glory to God!

> *Thank You, Jesus, for the living water*
> *that flows from Your throne into my*
> *life, filling me with salvation,*
> *healing, and revival. Amen.*
> —W. J. SEYMOUR 1906

Day 76

Receive Ye the Holy Ghost

*But the Comforter, which is the Holy
Ghost, whom the Father will send in my
name, he shall teach you all things.*
—JOHN 14:26

THE FIRST STEP in seeking the baptism
with the Holy Ghost is to have a clear
knowledge of the new birth in our souls,
which is the first work of grace and brings
everlasting life to our souls (Rom. 5:1). Every
one who repents and turns to the Lord Jesus
with faith in Him, receives forgiveness of sins.
Justification and regeneration are simulta-
neous. The pardoned sinner becomes a child
of God in justification.

The next step is to have a clear knowledge, by the Holy Spirit, of the second work
of grace wrought in our hearts by the power
of the blood and the Holy Ghost. "For by one
offering he hath perfected for ever them that
are sanctified. Whereof the Holy Ghost also is
a witness to us" (Heb. 10:14–15). We have

Christ, crowned and enthroned in our hearts, the tree of life. We have the brooks and streams of salvation flowing in our souls, but praise God, we can have the rivers (John 7:38–39). Christ is now given and being poured out upon all flesh. All races, nations, and tongues are receiving the baptism with the Holy Ghost and fire, according to the prophet Joel (2:28–32).

When we have a clear knowledge of justification and sanctification through the precious blood of Jesus Christ in our hearts, then we can be a recipient of the baptism with the Holy Ghost.

> *Lord, I bow to You, asking You to come into my life, filling and baptizing me with Your Spirit. Amen.*

—W. J. SEYMOUR
JANUARY 1906

Day 77

In a Divine Trance

He hath said, which heard the words of God, and . . . which saw the vision of the Almighty, falling into a trance, but having his eyes open.

—NUMBERS 24:16

WE KNOW that some look with disfavor upon falling under the power and many regard with suspicion visions and revelations. But how can any, who really believe in the Bible, doubt the genuineness of that which fully bears the marks of being of God, and which is also in fulfillment of the prophecies and promises of His Word? "Therefore I was left alone, and saw this great vision, and there remained no strength in me . . . and I became dumb. And behold, one like the similitude of the sons of men touched my lips: then I opened my mouth, and spake" (Dan. 10:8, 15–16).

Speaking of the coming of the Comforter, Christ says to the one who loves Him, "And I

will love him, and will manifest myself to him"
(John 14:21).

At Joppa the Spirit-baptized Peter fell into a
divine trance in which he saw the vision and
heard the voice that swept away his Jewish
exclusiveness, and sent him to Caesarea (Acts
10:9–20).

In 2 Corinthians 12:1, Paul says: "I will
come to visions and revelations of the Lord."
We also learn that when the Spirit shall begin
to be poured out upon all flesh in the last days,
they "shall prophesy" and "see visions" (Acts
2:17).

If you reject the real in these days, what will
you do with that of the same kind recorded in
the Scriptures? Will you throw away the Bible
because of unbelief to these mighty and mar-
velous workings of the Spirit in the present?

> *Lord, overwhelm me as You will, so*
> *that I may receive all that You desire*
> *to reveal to me. Amen.*

—MAY 1907

The Lord's Supper

The cup of blessing which we bless, is it not the communion of the blood of Christ? The bread which we break, is it not the communion of the body of Christ?
—1 Corinthians 10:16

According to Moses' law, the Lord Jesus ate the Passover with His disciples. It was now finished forever, as He shoved that table aside, and, after washing the disciples' feet, instituted the Lord's supper, the Christian Passover, the bread and the wine. The Passover was the very type of Jesus. It had a three-fold meaning: the sprinkled blood for *redemption;* the body of the Lamb eaten for *healing;* and the passing over the Red Sea which was a type of the blood of Jesus Christ that gives us *victory over all the powers of the enemy.*

The Passover supper always reminded the Jews of God's great love for them in delivering them out of Egyptian bondage.

"The Lord Jesus the same night in which he

was betrayed took bread: and when he had given thanks, he brake it, and said, Take, eat: this is my body, which is broken for you: this do in remembrance of me. After the same manner also he took the cup, when he had supped, saying, This cup is the new testament in my blood: this do ye, as oft as ye drink it, in remembrance of me. For as often as ye eat this bread, and drink this cup, ye do shew the Lord's death till he come" (1 Cor. 11:23–26). This ordinance points us to the coming of the Lord, our great deliverance, as the Passover was the deliverance of the children of Israel from Egypt.

Lord, as we partake of Your Last Supper in remembrance of You, remind us of the healing available to us through Your body and blood. Amen.

—SEPTEMBER 1907

Day 79

Spirit Baptism

*But ye shall be baptized with the Holy
Ghost not many days hence.*

—ACTS 1:5

THE BAPTISM of the Holy Spirit is power,
the understanding of His Word, and the
glory of God upon your life.

Whenever the Lord wants to play His
piano, He tunes up the harp and plays with
His own fingers, speaking or singing in any
language He wishes. The man that hears you
speak a message right from the throne, falls
down and seeks God, and gets up to report
that God is in you of a truth.

The baptism of the Holy Spirit makes you
more humble and filled with divine love.
Through Spirit baptism the graces and fruit of
the Spirit (Gal. 5:22–23) are manifest.

When you get the baptism with the Holy
Ghost, you will surely go up into the mount

with Christ. If you want to know what it is to praise God and have the joy of the Lord in your soul that flows like a mighty river, tarry and get your personal Pentecost.

He keeps the rivers flowing in your soul that you may be fit for irrigation wherever you go. Jesus said, "He that believeth on me, as the scripture hath said, out of his belly shall flow rivers of living water. (But this spake he of the Spirit, which they that believe on him should receive)" (John 7:38–39).

> *Flood me, Oh, Spirit, with Your baptism that Your grace and fruit might be manifested in my life. Amen.*
>
> —MAY 1908

Day 80

Repentance and Prayer

If we confess our sins, he is faithful and just to forgive us our sins, and to cleanse us from all unrighteousness.

—1 JOHN 1:9

YOU MUST FIRST repent before you pray to God, because you must have the Word of God in your heart. God heareth not sinners. But when one has godly sorrow, and prays, he is no more a sinner.

We must have Christ (the Word) in us before we can have power with God. We only have power with God through Jesus. He puts the Spirit in us that He might recognize Himself.

Lord Jesus, I repent and confess my sins. Hear my prayers. Amen.

—MAY 1908

Day 81

Free From Sin

Whosoever is born of God doth not commit sin.

—1 JOHN 3:9

THE WORD OF GOD is the seed that remains in us. Christ sanctified our souls. He is the seed. Praise God for the blood of Jesus Christ that cleanses and sanctifies from all sin. Sin is sin. There are not white, little, or black sins before God. It takes the same blood of Jesus Christ to cleanse us from all sin. God never saves anyone in sin *to* sin, but He saves *from* sin. Bless His holy name!

We can live a life free from sin if we will only believe God and obey His precious Word. All provision in the power of the Holy Ghost is made for us to live a life free from sin.

Lord, empower me in Your Spirit to live and completely free from sin. Amen.

—APRIL 1907

Day 82

From His Well

*But whosoever drinketh of the water that
I shall give him shall never thirst.*

—JOHN 4:14

THERE ARE MANY wells today, but they are
dry. There are many hungry souls today
that are empty. So let us come to Jesus and
take Him at His Word, and we will find wells
of salvation, and will be able to draw waters
out of the well of salvation, for Jesus is that
well.

Jesus was weary from a long journey as He
sat on the well in Samaria where a woman
came to draw water. He asked her for a drink.
She answered, "How is it that thou, being a
Jew, askest drink of me, which am a woman of
Samaria? for the Jews have no dealings with
the Samaritans" Jesus said, "If thou knewest
the gift of God, and who it is that saith to thee,
Give me to drink; thou wouldest have asked of

him, and he would have given thee living water" (John 4:9–10).

Oh, how sweet it was to see Jesus, the Lamb of God who takes away the sin of the world. That great sacrifice God gave to a lost, dying, and benighted world, sitting on the well and talking with the woman. Jesus was so gentle, meek, and kind that it gave her an appetite to talk further with Him, until He got into her secret and uncovered her life. Then she was pricked in heart, confessed her sins, and received pardon. Beyond all of this, she received the well of salvation in her heart.

Flow out of me, Oh, well, with living
water from the river of God. Amen.

—W. J. SEYMOUR
NOVEMBER 1906

Day 83

Sermon From a Dress

Though your sins be as scarlet, they shall be as white as snow; though they be red like crimson, they shall be as wool.
—ISAIAH 1:18

THE LORD makes His truth so plain that a wayfaring man, though a fool, shall not err therein. You have all seen a dirty dress washed. But you never saw a person take a dirty dress and iron it. And you never saw them take a dress and wash and iron it all at once. And you never saw a person put on a dress and iron it.

The dirty dress represents a person in sin. Your righteousness is filthy rags. "Though your sins be as scarlet, they shall be as white as snow." When you get the dress washed, that represents a justified experience. When the dress is washed and on the line, you rejoice because the washing is through.

But the clothes need something else before

they are ready to wear. What do they need? Why, they need to be ironed. You would be ashamed to take the clothes off the line and wear them without ironing. Jesus would be ashamed to present you before the Father if you were not sanctified. But when you are sanctified, He is not ashamed to call you brethren. Christ gave Himself for His church that He might wash it and present it without spot or wrinkle (Eph. 5:27). So we must let Him iron out all the wrinkles.

The Holy Ghost is a free gift. It is the promise of the Father to the soul that is sanctified. You do not have to repent to get the Holy Ghost, but you must be washed clean and whiter than snow.

> *Oh God, how I desire to be presented before Your throne without spot or wrinkle. Iron me that I might be perfect in Your sight. Amen.*
>
> —OPHELIA WILEY
> OCTOBER 1906

Day 84

Receiving the Holy Ghost

*And when he [Jesus] had said this, he
breathed on them, and saith unto them,
Receive ye the Holy Ghost.*

—JOHN 20:22

GOD HAS TOLD His children to be witnesses,
and the most convincing evidence is testi-
mony of personal knowledge.

I dropped into the meetings on Azusa Street
some time in April, having heard that some
people were speaking in tongues, as they did
on the day of Pentecost.

At first the meeting seemed a very tame
affair to me. As I was indoctrinated in the
second blessing being the baptism with the
Holy Ghost, I branded the teaching as
heretical, not going to the meetings for some
time.

In fact, I could not stay away. My heart
began to break up, and soon I was going from
one person to another, asking them to forgive

me for harsh words and criticism.

I began to earnestly seek for the Lord to have His way with me. The Holy Ghost showed me that I must be clay in the Potter's hands, an empty vessel before the Lord.

On a Saturday morning I awoke and stretched my arms toward heaven and asked God to fill me with the Holy Ghost. My arms began to tremble, and soon I was shaken violently by a great power. About thirty hours afterwards, while sitting in the meeting on Azusa Street, I felt my throat and tongue begin to move, without any effort on my part. Soon I began to stutter and then out came a distinct language which I could hardly restrain.

> *Spirit of God, fill me with Your baptism of tongues, fire, joy, and laughter. Amen.*

—G. A. COOK
NOVEMBER 1906

Day 85

Gifts of the Spirit

Now concerning spiritual gifts, brethren,
I would not have you ignorant.
—1 Corinthians 12:1

PAUL WAS SPEAKING to the Corinthian Church. They were like Christ's people everywhere today. Many of His people do not know their privileges in this blessed gospel. The Gospel of Christ is the power of God unto salvation to every one who believes (Rom. 1:16). And in order that we might know His power, we must forever abide in the Word of God, that we may have the precious fruit of the Spirit, and not only the fruits but the precious gifts the Father has for His little ones.

Many people say today that tongues are the least gift of any that the Lord can give, and they do not need it. They ask, "What good is it to us?" But 1 Corinthians 14:1 clearly declares, "Follow after charity, and desire spiritual gifts." Charity means divine love without which we will never be able to enter heaven. Gifts all will fail, but divine love will last through all eternity. In the same verse Paul says, "Desire . . . rather that ye may prophesy." That is to say, preach in your own tongue, which will build up the saints and the church.

Praise God, every gift He gives is a good gift. It is very blessed, for when the Lord gets ready, He can speak in any language He chooses to speak. You ask, "Is not prophecy the best gift?" Prophecy is the best gift to the church, for it builds up the saints and edifies them and exalts them to higher things in the Lord Jesus. May we all use our gift to the glory of God and not worship the gift. The Lord gives us power to use it to His own glory and honor.

Lord, I desire Your spiritual gifts so that the body of Christ may be edified through me. Amen.

—W. J. SEYMOUR
JANUARY 1907

Day 86

Unlocked by Prayer

Wherefore, let him that speaketh in an unknown tongue pray that he may interpret.

—1 CORINTHIANS 14:13

GOD HAS NOT GIVEN you, through the power of the Holy Ghost, that which is no language or has no meaning. You need not hunt around for somebody to interpret. That is as bad as Saul going to the witch of Endor. People may tell you it is some kind of gibberish you are speaking, but you know that it means something because the Holy Ghost gave it to you. So let him that speaks in an unknown tongue pray that he may interpret. The interpretation is unlocked by prayer.

I am glad the Lord has some things the devil cannot find out. If not, anyone could unlock the mysteries of Christ.

In the Corinthian church, the tongues sounded so sweet that they all wanted to speak in tongues, and the Lord showed them that love was the theme. In 1 Corinthians 14, Paul was trying to teach government and wisdom to the church. They were very zealous, and the whole company of baptized believers wanted to talk in tongues at once.

Paul said: "I would that ye all spake with tongues, but rather that ye prophesied" (1 Cor. 14:5). Paul wants us to go forward and get deeper things yet. He said he spoke in tongues more than others, putting himself with them that they might see that he was not fighting the gift.

> *Spirit of God, speak through me and interpret all that You say to the glory of God. Amen.*

—MAY 1907

Day 87

Water Baptism

Therefore we are buried with him by baptism into death: that like as Christ was raised up from the dead by the glory of the Father, even so we also should walk in newness of life.
—ROMANS 6:4

WE BELIEVE in water baptism by immersion because Jesus commanded it after His resurrection. Mark 16:16, "He that believeth and is baptized shall be saved." Notice these teachings from the Word.

- "And Jesus, when he was baptized, went up straightway out of the water" (Matt. 3:16).
- "And he commanded the chariot to stand still: and they went down both into the water, both Philip and the eunuch; and he baptized him. And when they were come up out of the water, the Spirit of the Lord

caught away Philip, that the eunuch saw him no more: and he went on his way rejoicing" (Acts 8:38–39).

Baptism is not a saving ordinance, but it is essential because it is a command of our Lord (Mark 16:16).

- "Repent, and be baptized everyone of you in the name of Jesus Christ for the remission of sins" (Acts 2:38).
- Baptism is "not the putting away of the filth of the flesh, but the answer of a good conscience toward God" (1 Pet. 3:21).

Thank You, Lord, for providing baptism as a means to obey You and witness to the work of Your Spirit in me. Amen.

Day 88

He Will Speak

Quench not the Spirit. Despise not proph-esyings. Prove all things; hold fast that which is good.

—1 THESSALONIANS 5:19–21

SOMEONE MAY say, "If you can speak in tongues, let me hear you." Don't you ever try to do that. The Holy Ghost will never speak in that way. It is not ye that speak but the Holy Ghost, and He will speak when He chooses.

"It is by My Spirit," saith the Lord (Zech. 4:6). When singing or speaking in tongues, your mind does not take any part in it. He wants you to pray for the interpretation, so that you can speak with the Spirit and with the understanding also (1 Cor. 14:16).

Holy Spirit, speak through my thoughts, words, and actions. Amen.

—MAY 1908

Day 89

Keep Your Eyes on Jesus

Looking unto Jesus the author and finisher of our faith.

—HEBREWS 12:2

KEEP YOUR EYES on Jesus and not on the manifestations of the Holy Ghost. Do not seek something more than someone else. The Lord God wants you humble as a baby.

If you set your eyes on manifestations and signs, you are likely to get a counterfeit. What you really want to seek is more holiness and more of God.

Jesus, it is You that I seek—not more from You, only more of You. Amen.

—JANUARY 1908

Day 90

Unity in the Blood

That they all may be one; as thou, Father, art in me, and I in thee, that they also may be one in us: that the world may believe that thou hast sent me.

—JOHN 17:21

It is the blood of Jesus that brings fellowship among the Christian family. "But if we walk in the light, as he is in the light, we have fellowship one with another" (1 John 1:7).

The blood of Jesus is the strongest bond of fellowship in the world. It makes all races and nations into one common family in the Lord. The Holy Ghost is the leader and He makes all one through the blood of Jesus, just as He prayed.

Lord, in Your blood make us one in Your family. Amen.

—APRIL 1907

CREATION HOUSE PRESENTS . . .

The Charisma Classic Devotional Series

- *The Original Smith Wigglesworth Devotional*

- *The Original John G. Lake Devotional*

- *The Original Maria Woodworth-Etter Devotional*

These books are ninety-day devotionals containing the original, edited words of Smith Wigglesworth, John G. Lake, and Maria Woodworth-Etter. Each devotion includes a scripture, a daily reading, and a daily prayer.

To order any of the devotionals
listed on this page, contact:

CREATION HOUSE
600 Rinehart Road
Lake Mary, Florida 32746
800.283.8494